KU-769-417

the
SPIRIT
of
SUCCESS

Margaret and Robin

the
SPIRIT
of
SUCCESS

"Stedfast and Sure"!

How to connect your heart to your head in work and life

norman
drummond

with all good wishes

Norman Drummond.

HODDER
MOBIUS

Hodder & Stoughton

Copyright © 2004 by by Norman Drummond

First published in Great Britain in 2004 by Hodder and Stoughton
A division of Hodder Headline
This paperback edition published in 2005

The right of Norman Drummond to be identified as the Author of
the Work has been asserted by him in accordance with the
Copyright, Designs and Patents Act 1988

A Mobius paperback

2

All rights reserved. No part of this publication may be
reproduced, stored in a retrieval system, or transmitted,
in any form or by any means without the prior written
permission of the publisher, nor be otherwise circulated in
any form of binding or cover other than that in which it
is published and without a similar condition being imposed
on the subsequent purchaser

A CIP catalogue record for this title is available from the British Library

ISBN 0340 82933 8

Typeset in Sabon by Palimpsest Book Production Limited,
Polmont, Stirlingshire
Printed and bound in Great Britain by
Clays Ltd, St Ives plc

Hodder Headline's policy is to use papers that are natural, renewable and
recyclable products and made from wood grown in sustainable forests.
The logging and manufacturing processes are expected to conform to
the environmental regulations of the country of origin

Hodder and Stoughton Ltd
A division of Hodder Headline
338 Euston Road
London NW1 3BH

To those essential qualities of Courage, Kindness, Devotion, Serenity, Integrity and Dignity, in other words Elizabeth, Andrew, Maggie, Marie Clare, Christian and Ruaraidh

With love.

'And now these three remain: Faith, Hope and Love. But the greatest of these is Love.'

1 Corinthians 13, 13

acknowledgements

So many people have been so very kind and encouraging to me over the years and without these words of kindness and encouragement along the way this book would have remained in my mind as an occasional stream of consciousness.

A loving and reliable home life must surely be the best start for any child and in that regard I was assuredly blessed. I can still hear Mascagni's *Cavelleria Rusticana* being played at full blast by my father whilst my ever-caring and capable mother urged him to turn it down so as to let the children get to sleep! Yet at a recent concert in Glasgow given by the immaculate Andrea Bocelli I heard again through *Cavelleria Rusticana* my father's voice saying to me 'Go on now, you can do it'.

Perhaps that phrase rediscovered more than thirty years since my father's sudden heart attack and passing is the key to understanding and benefiting from *The Spirit of Success*. It is only when your heart is connected to your head that you can truly become the person you were created to be.

In this particular journey towards "The Spirit of Success: How to connect your head to your heart in work and life" I am of course indebted to my family, to my outstanding personal assistant, Wilma Shalliday, and to my delightful editor, Caro Handley, with whom it has been such a pleasure to work. The leadership of Rowena Webb at Hodder & Stoughton has been inspiring and I am so grateful to Rowena and her team.

Yet it was my agent, Kay McCauley of the Pimlico Agency in New York, who really got me started, helping me to realise that I could write and so help others in at times remarkable ways. Kay also taught me that this could be fun. Her sense of humour subconsciously reminded me of my father's sense of humour and fun and with it his words to me 'Go on, you can do it'.

I trust and pray that those transcendent words will now inspire many readers to 'Go on' because, when your heart is connected to your head, 'you can do it'!

contents

Looking Back and Moving Forward

i In the nineteenth century three of my four great-grandfathers became entrepreneurs, setting up their own businesses in Scotland. Each of those great-grandfathers began with very little. Each was determined to better himself and to provide for his family, and was not afraid to work hard and take every opportunity which came along. The companies they began 140 years ago are still thriving today. They have provided thousands of people with employment and over the years they have shaped our family's life and attitude. One of those companies remains in the family and is now employing a fifth generation.

It was a wonderful legacy. But my great-grandfathers passed on more than just the companies they founded. They passed on the values and beliefs which led to their success in the first place and which kept their businesses working so well. All three men were passionate egalitarians who believed that we have our humanity in common. They hated pomposity and were always willing to admit their own mistakes and to learn from them. They were self-reliant men who also believed in clear leadership and in showing respect and kindness towards those who worked for and with them. The message passed down by them is that hard work will reap benefits, both materially and spiritually, and that the choices you make in life and the way you live and work will have profound consequences.

These are the messages which I grew up with and which I have taken into my own working life. As a coach, mentor and mediator working on both sides of the Atlantic I see many different kinds of businesses and the people who run them. And I have come to believe that many of the values and ideals my great-grandfathers held so dear have been lost and need to be rediscovered. Of course we can't turn the clock back, nor would we want to. Many things have changed for the better since my great-grandfathers' days. But the beliefs and values they held in their working lives are still very relevant.

Too many of the people I see in workplaces are simply functioning – getting through the day, covering their backs and following the company line. The board rooms and offices of the Western world are full of fragmented souls who no longer know who they are and who have lost their purpose. Many of them work long hours for great material rewards but are weighed down by anxieties, pressures and unhappiness.

On a recent trip to the United States I met an editor from the *Wall Street Journal*. He told me a story about an acquaintance of his who had concentrated single-mindedly on his business interests for many years. When the time came, in his late forties, to sell up and benefit from the fruits of his labours, this man really had no idea who he was or what he wished to do with his life. In fact, said the editor, if you talked to him about his soul he would probably look for the fish section on a restaurant menu. His years of hard labour had brought him money, but no real insight, satisfaction or happiness. There are many men and women like this who have lost their sense of direction and who don't really know what they want or what matters most to them. They believe that material rewards define their success, yet they have no sense of joy and take no real pleasure in what they do.

Then there are those who run, or suffer under, unhappy regimes at work. Set-ups where people are fuelled by fear of failure rather than the joy of success, where being humiliated is common and encouragement barely exists, and where individuals are interested only in their own gain and not that of others or the organisation as a whole. When this is the case, no one benefits. Staff turnover is high and morale low, productivity suffers and things go wrong. There are still many organisations which are run in this way, but change is in the air. As people throughout the Western world discover that bigger isn't necessarily better, that money doesn't buy happiness and that a life spent toeing the company line doesn't bring insight or fulfilment, they are looking for a different way of doing things and for something more.

But what is this something more? I believe that to find real satisfaction, a deeper sense of purpose and genuine success we need to begin by looking inward. Too many of us rely on what is outside ourselves – material rewards and feedback from others – while neglecting the resources we have inside. Our ability truly to know ourselves, to be self-reliant, to trust our own judgement, to stand apart from the crowd and to make independent decisions often resembles a wasted muscle. This muscle needs developing and exercising until it becomes a resource that we can rely on in any situation.

Alongside greater self-reliance and self-knowledge we need to see the bigger picture. Not just our own needs and wants but those of the people we work with and those of the organisations we work in. We need to establish values and working practices that benefit every person in a company as well as others outside it, no matter how large or small the company is. Every member of an organisation should feel that the organisation as a whole matters, and that they as an individual matter as much as everyone else. Too often the fat cats at the top cream off the benefits while those in the middle or at the bottom are left underpaid, unrecognised and frustrated. When this happens people are encouraged to trample over others to make it to the top, and once there they care little for anyone else. But if we leave our sense of integrity behind on the way to the top, the shine of success can suddenly seem dull and grey. In a company where everyone matters, everyone can benefit and everyone can feel good about who they are and what they do, whether that is making the tea or chairing the board. A shared sense of purpose, of humour, of achievement and of enjoyment is the greatest spur of all to full productivity and loyal, happy employees.

To create great organisations you need great individuals. People who are successful yet who want more than just material success. People who believe in the possible and who have vision. Who put people before projects and who still complete their projects successfully. Such people have high standards of behaviour: they are kind without being soft and firm without being cruel. They are not afraid to make mistakes and to own up to them, and are consistently able to inspire and encourage others. Above all, they stand out for their humanity and for their ability to use their heads while not forgetting their hearts. Every one of us has the ability to be such a person. The novelist and colonial administrator John Buchan once wrote: 'Our task is not to put the greatness back into humanity but to elicit it, for the greatness is there already.' Each of us has our own unique inner greatness. The challenge in life is to bring out this greatness and use it in the best possible way.

This book is a guide to the art of greatness, a step-by-step manual on how to explore and expand your own resources, abilities and potential. It is based on the premise that to be truly successful you must first look inwards and get to know yourself. Discovering who you really are and where you are going is vital to living and working in a creative, fulfilling and productive way. Using questions, exercises, illustrations and simple techniques I offer ways of developing your self-knowledge and self-reliance in order to work more effectively, produce better results and manage your life in rewarding and fulfilling ways. I look at ways of resolving issues such as anxiety, pressure, overwork, managing difficult colleagues and meeting impossible demands. I also explore ways to maintain an ideal work/life balance, to create a happy and successful working environment and to deal simply and effectively with workplace problems.

I want to give you a whole new way of looking at things, literally from the inside out. I want to help you create a working life worth working and a life worth living. Because no one should settle for anything less.

chapter 1

Three Vital Questions

I was once asked to speak to a group of oil executives at a dinner in Aberdeen, the oil capital of Scotland. These were internationally successful entrepreneurs and company executives who had gathered from around the world, and I knew they expected me to chat about various aspects of their industry. But this particular evening I decided to go out on a limb and try something a little different. I asked them three very simple but very important questions:

- Who are you?
- Why are you living and working in the way that you are?
- What might you yet become and do with your life?

I could see the shock on their faces. Being asked to question their lives, their choices and their direction was not on the menu. These were men and women who were driven by position and status, and who didn't expect to be confronted with life's more fundamental issues over their cheese and port.

I wondered whether the questions I had asked would be dismissed as ridiculous. But the warm applause I received when I finished was followed by a generous handshake from a number of executives who told me, 'Thank you. I needed to be asked those questions – you've really made me think tonight.' The next morning as I was checking out of the hotel a woman came up to me and said, 'That was the first real appraisal my husband has had in twenty years in the oil industry.'

Those three questions are the ones all of us, no matter what our life and career choices, need to ask ourselves regularly if we are to work in an ethical, human and fulfilling way. It is not enough simply to turn up and do the job, whether you are the new apprentice or the chairman of the company. You need to know where you are going, what matters to you, why you chose this job and what you want to do with your future. You need to think about what kind of person you are at work, how others see you and what you achieve – not just on the production line, but in human terms too.

Let me ask you to look at these three questions in more detail and to think about your own answers.

WHO ARE YOU?

This is the most important of the three questions and the hardest to answer. It requires inner strength, courage and honesty to take a long, hard look at yourself and ask fundamental questions, but if you're willing to do this the rewards are great.

In his poem 'Build me a son' General Douglas MacArthur says: 'Build me a child . . . that will know that to know himself is the foundation stone of knowledge.' When you know and accept who you are, when there are no dark corners of yourself which you avoid, you become a fully centred and grounded human being. You are able to 'fill your own shoes', feeling a comfortable sense of your own presence; and you know and understand what true self-acceptance is. When you know who you are you can:

Like yourself
Which means putting aside self-criticism, conceit and false modesty and simply appreciating your own qualities and the effort you put in.

Take your time
And keep to a pace which feels comfortable and right for you, whatever pace others around you may choose.

Trust yourself to cope in any situation
No matter how great the pressure or how tough the circumstances, you will be able to call on the qualities you have to see you through.

Stick to your own belief system
Knowing your own beliefs and keeping to them, even when others doubt or disagree, is the basis of self-knowledge.

Stay the course despite the difficulties
Keeping on track towards your goal and refusing to be diverted or defeated.

Bypass obstacles in your way
By moving skilfully round them or shifting them without damage to others.

the Spirit of Success

Face whatever comes with calm and confidence
Because your inner core is strong and trustworthy and you know you need not rely on others to tell you who you are or what to do.

These are the qualities of the truly authentic person, the man or woman who is neither rigidly inflexible nor marshmallow-soft but who is able to steer a course which is clear and focused, yet still gives value to the feelings and opinions of others.

Those who don't know who they are often fall at the first fence, or suffer painful consequences. Here are some of the pitfalls which can catch out the man or woman who has no real sense of themselves.

Borrowing Models

Those who don't know themselves are not able to be authentic. In order to be true to yourself you need to know what makes you tick and what forces and beliefs determine your behaviour. Those who don't know these things and aren't comfortable with themselves usually borrow models for their behaviour. For instance, if there is a task to be done, such as a speech to make, they might think of someone whom they have seen do it well and attempt to model themselves on this person, borrowing tired jokes and stories. Their performance will come across as insincere, nervous or unconvincing.

A large insurance company engaged a British sporting hero to speak at a prestigious company dinner. The head of human resources took the sportsman out for dinner to discuss the event, and asked him to speak from the heart during his speech, rather than to provide a list of sporting stories. But the sportsman had no idea what the HR man meant. His speech was stilted and heavily rehearsed, he floundered halfway through and then became grumpy when questions were asked. This man, for all his sporting achievements, had no idea who he was and functioned according to a model he had borrowed.

Using Props

Many people go through life with an array of props, which in business terms often include a generous benefits package, a top-of-the-range car and a big pension. They see themselves as successful, basing their definition of success on these material benefits. Acquiring and maintaining these benefits often involves working ridiculous hours and neglecting their families, homes and dreams.

A wealthy, successful client was so busy building up his rapidly expanding business that he simply didn't notice his wife's loneliness and unhappiness. He planned a retirement in Spain and dreamed of sitting out his latter years under a beach umbrella with a long, cool drink, his wife by his side. The trouble was, he was so busy focusing on the material benefits and the end result that he missed what was happening in his life now, right under his nose. Only when his wife announced that she was leaving him for a man who came to do some repair work on their house did he realise that in focusing on the props he had lost what really mattered most to him.

Material benefits are fine, as long as they are no more than a pleasant extra and not the end goal of life. Those who spend every moment in hot pursuit of purely material success don't know why they are doing so, because they never stop for long enough to find out. They are too busy papering over the cracks of their existence by presenting a glossy exterior to the world. I sometimes look at the great and the grand, wearing glamorous outfits as they arrive at some function or other in a stretch limo, and wonder how many of them are truly happy and comfortable with themselves. After all, the inner strength of the personality doesn't depend on the size of your income, house or car.

Lacking Balance

Sometimes people are so busy with certain aspects of their lives that they are in denial about others. Knowing who you are is about facing every aspect of yourself and your life, even the toughest parts. Sometimes it can take a painful experience to teach us who we are.

> The newly appointed director of a promising theatre company was spending a great deal of time at work and arriving home late each evening. So upset was his wife that one morning there was a blazing row overheard by their young son. That evening the theatre director arrived home late to complete darkness save one light in an upstairs room, his son's. When the key was turned in the door the young boy came rushing downstairs and jumped into his father's arms. Years later the father reminded his son of this loving gesture. He described it as one of the best moments of his life. His son, now a young adult, replied somewhat unexpectedly, 'And the worst moment of my life was when I got 90% in my maths paper and instead of congratulating me you asked me what happened with the other ten marks. Since then I've never asked you for anything and I've never let you down'. The father was humbled. He realised how tough and relentless he had been towards his son – just as his father had been to him. He understood, at last, that encouragement, approval and love might have gone so much further, and he promised himself he would put things right.

This father had come to understand that he set impossible standards for himself and for his children, and in doing this he had missed out on so much love, fun and pleasure with them. He had lived a life out of balance, concentrating on one aspect – the drive to succeed – at the cost of all others.

FINDING OUT WHO YOU ARE

So how do we find out who we really are? Firstly by asking the most important question of all, the one which is at the root of all else we become and do.

Where Do I Come From?

There is an ancient Celtic proverb which runs: 'In order to understand where you are going you have to understand where you come from.' If you are willing to be painfully honest in finding the answer to this question, it will take you forward and provide answers for the rest of your life. Finding out where you come from means looking back at your childhood, your home, school and parents, or those who brought you up. Here lie the clues to present-day beliefs and behaviour.

My father was born into a prosperous household in Greenock, near Glasgow. His father was the Provost (Mayor) and he and my grandmother were devoted to civic duty. My grandparents were good people who did their best, as most parents do. But the demands of their lives meant that my father grew up with very little attention or physical affection. This created patterns of behaviour which impacted on us, his own children. He could never believe that he was loved or successful, and because of this he was never satisfied with himself or with others. The result was that we longed to please him and win his approval. When he died young, at fifty-one, we could only hope that he had known how much we loved him.

Understanding this was a great help to me in recognising my own flaws and deciding to do things differently with my own children. No matter how successful and talented a person is, if they don't understand the legacy of their childhood they will hold on to the anxieties, insecurities

13

and limiting beliefs which they took on as children.

Nine in ten of the clients I coach have worries based on fear of failure. I see heads of companies, chief executives and senior managers who, in the eyes of the world, have done very well for themselves. Yet they don't see it that way themselves. They suffer from anxiety, pressure, guilt and fear. They often come to me with a host of business issues they want to resolve. However, when I encourage them to dig a little deeper we find that underneath the 'business issues' are personal worries and fears.

> One client, a woman who headed a successful fashion business, told me that she was constantly worried about money. Despite her high income and good pension provision she feared losing it all, and her fear was making her life miserable. When I asked her to tell me about her background she revealed that her father had lost his small business and gone bankrupt, causing the family to move home and send her to a different school. The family had gone on to prosper again and she had forgotten this bleak period, which happened when she was only seven. But it had clearly left her with fears which she was still carrying around.

By asking you to examine where you come from I am not suggesting you go into therapy or spend endless hours analysing. Simply that you do a little research on yourself, look back and make connections between the past and the present. These connections are of great value. Current behaviours, beliefs, ambitions and practices can be explained in terms of the past, and this is a vital and important starting point for knowing who you really are.

Exercise

Spend ten minutes writing down the following:

- Five things I remember about my father
- Five things I remember about my mother

- Five words I would use to sum up my childhood
- Five words others would use to sum me up

Try to remember one or two incidents from your childhood and how you behaved and reacted at the time. Now look at any links which emerge. You will be surprised at how much this brief exercise reveals. If you find it useful you can go on to lengthen the lists – you will undoubtedly spot more connections.

Let Go of the Guard's Van

So many people are weighed down by the baggage of the past. Their fears, regrets, guilt and shame hang round their necks like millstones, taking away from the pleasure they might have in other aspects of their lives. I often see very successful men and women who are deeply worried because they feel they've lost their sense of integrity by doing something they're ashamed of – an affair, a hurtful act of some kind or a dubious business deal.

I call this the Guard's Van. If life were a train this would be the van at the back, carrying all sorts of odds and ends and trailing along wherever the rest goes. And a large part of the journey, for many of us, would be spent revisiting the Guard's Van to remind ourselves of the contents. There's an old film called *North West Frontier* in which the characters are taking a train across the desert. Kenneth More, playing the hero, is helping a small group of people, mostly women and children, to escape from a hostile situation. But the train is too heavy to go on, so More unhooks the coupling which holds the guard's van to the rest of the train and lets it go. Unburdened, the train moves on much more smoothly and swiftly to its destination.

So many of us need to let go of that Guard's Van we're dragging around. The sense of relief and of freedom it brings is immense. But many people find it hard to let go – after all, they have been attached to this van full of misery and regret for many years. So I often suggest that, if there is something to be put right, people should just go ahead and do it.

> A high-achieving woman manager told me she felt a lot of guilt about the engagement she had broken off. Her fiancé had been heartbroken and had felt he would never meet anyone else. She had broken off the relationship in a rather brutal and thoughtless way, and she regretted it. She decided to write to her ex-fiancé, even though several years had passed. She said that she hoped he was happy, and apologised for the way she had hurt him. Even though she never heard from him, writing the letter made her feel she could put the whole thing behind her and move on.

This is exactly what we all need to do – move on. None of us is perfect: we've all made mistakes, done things we regret and hurt people. Sometimes we are lucky enough to be able to put things right. But mostly we can't even do that. All we can do is learn what our mistakes have to teach us and let them go. Life is not meant to be perfect – it is often a series of imperfections. The losses and defeats we have and the mistakes we make are all part of our journey, and without them we would be poorer. The challenge is in the way we cope with these experiences.

So how do you let go? Simply by deciding that you will. Make the decision today to let go of the Guard's Van. Release the anger, guilt, regret and shame you may be carrying. Feel your shoulders lighten as the burden drops.

Knowing Yourself

The key to knowing yourself is self-acceptance. If you can feel good about yourself while accepting that you aren't perfect, have made mistakes in the past and continue to get it wrong some of the time, then you have come a long way. Many people recognise that they are loving, but don't see themselves as loved and lovable. To feel unlovable is a form of self-rejection which can only make us feel unhappy. If you accept that you are lovable you will take a huge stride forward towards self-knowledge.

Exercise

Ask yourself the following five questions:

- Do I act in a way which is consistent with my belief system?
- Do I trust myself?
- Do I stay the course, even when facing a difficult situation?
- Do I have inner strength?
- Do I like myself?

If you are able to answer 'yes' to all these questions, you are beginning to know yourself better. If there are any to which you answered 'no', this will indicate the areas you might need to adjust.

Remember that if you act in accordance with your belief system you will always be consistent, self-reliant and honest. If you act with integrity you will be trustworthy. If you call on your courage you will always stay the course in the face of difficulties, obstacles and objections. If you follow your own judgement, even when it flies in the face of others' opinions, you will have inner strength. And if you do all of these things consistently, you will like yourself.

WHY ARE YOU LIVING AND WORKING IN THE WAY THAT YOU ARE?

This question is very closely tied in with the first (see p. 8). If you know who you are then you know why you're doing what you're doing. But it bears some examination of its own as well.

Most of us don't often question what we are doing. We feel that life has led us along certain paths, that we have taken certain opportunities or been directed by others, and that is how we have landed where we are today. We might call it luck, fate or just circumstance. We might be pretty happy with it, or we might feel there are things we would like to change, but how often do we say, 'What choices brought me here and why do I stay?' Yet everything we do in life is the result of choice, either conscious or unconscious.

Exercise

Ask yourself now why you are in your present job. Here are some possible answers for you to consider:

- I want to be seen to be a success
- I want to please others (family, friends, bosses)
- This is what my family always planned for me
- I was good at it so it seemed natural
- I like the material rewards
- I want security

Now ask yourself whether the answers you have given satisfy you. Are you doing what you are doing because you love it and you would rather be doing this than anything else? Or is it a compromise – something you have settled for rather than a first choice?

> A man who had worked in a bank for twenty years came to see me feeling very low. He hated his job and always had. When I asked why he was doing this particular job he told me he had gone to work in the bank because his brother had gone there before him. His family felt it was a good job that offered security, and he had gone along with their wishes.

> Now, after twenty years, he had lost heart and simply functioned at work,
> much preferring to be at home with his wife. When we explored the kinds
> of things he loved doing he realised he would like to work with children,
> and he then found a job in which he could help underprivileged young
> people. As he made the changes in his life he no longer felt low – he was
> like a neglected plant which has suddenly been given water, and he became
> lighter in spirit and happier.

When asking yourself why you are living and working in
the way that you are there are a couple of useful exercises you
can try which may help you to see your situation more clearly.

Exercise: the Outer Body Experience

This is a useful tool to use in all kinds of situations. It
involves mentally standing back from yourself and observ-
ing, as though you were a fly on the wall. You need to be
willing to detach from yourself and to see yourself as others
might see you, but it is well worth the effort. Through doing
this, for a few minutes at a time, you can create a more
objective view of your life and the way you choose to live
it. Watch yourself as you interact with others, deal with
problems and go through your day, and notice what is of
value and what might be usefully changed.

The Mirror Exercise

This is a similar exercise which is also useful when taking
a long, hard look at your life. Stand in front of a large
mirror, so close that all you can see is your face – and even
the details of your face are blurred. Now take a step back,
bringing your face into focus and opening up the scenario
a little. Step back a couple of paces further and suddenly
you can see the whole of yourself, and the environment
around you. You can pick out the detail and see yourself
in the context of the room you are in.

I use this exercise with coaching clients in the drawing room of Drummond International, where the wallpaper has a starred design. When clients stand close to the mirror the wallpaper looks blurred to them, but as they step back the pattern becomes clear, representing the stellar opportunities in their lives. This is a great illustration of what happens when we are so involved in the minutiae of our lives that we fail to stand back and see the whole picture.

Standing back is a valuable thing to do and will help you to answer the question: why are you doing what you are doing? And the answers you give to this question will lead you on to the third question.

WHAT MIGHT YOU YET BECOME AND DO WITH YOUR LIFE?

What hopes, dreams and plans do you have for the future? What great possibilities lie within you and have yet to be explored and enjoyed? This question opens up, for each one of us, the wonderful world of choice. Everything we do in life, every move we make, every turn we take, is a choice. No matter how much it feels as though you are at the whim of others' choices, or are swept along by the tide of life, there is still always a choice to be made, even if it is simply the attitude with which you approach life.

Choose Your Attitude

Your choice of attitude is the most important choice you can make, because your attitude will play a large part in determining the outcome of any situation. A positive attitude is far more likely to result in a positive outcome, no matter how difficult the circumstances, and a negative attitude is likely to result in a negative outcome, even when circumstances seem to be on our side. Each of us has known people who seem always to see the bright side of life and who aren't daunted by difficulties, and others who see problems ahead, no matter how many good things come their way. We have the choice, every day, to face what comes with dignity, courage, humour and trust, or to face it with doubt, fear, anxiety and suspicion.

When Sir Tom Farmer, founder of the Kwik-Fit chain, began to expand internationally, he came across the following unattributed quote. He gave me a copy, which is now framed on my office wall.

> The longer I live the more I realise the impact of attitude on life. Attitude is more important than the past, than education, money or circumstances, than failures or successes, than what other people think, say, or do. It is more important than appearance, giftedness, or skill.
>
> The remarkable thing is that you have a choice every day regarding the attitude you will embrace for that day.
>
> We cannot change our past . . . we cannot change the fact that people will act in a certain way. We cannot change the inevitable . . . the only thing we can do is play on the one string we have, and that is our attitude.

In the most difficult of circumstances, attitude can make all the difference in the world.

> Two Black Watch soldiers had been friends since they were children, growing up in the same village and going to the same school. They both joined up at the first opportunity in the Second World War and were assigned to the same section of the same company. During a battle, as they fought side by side the odds became so heavy that they were ordered to retreat. As they did so, they operated the buddy/buddy system, one moves while one waits and then the other moves while the first one waits. As they moved back through the lines one of the friends was wounded, and as he fell he told his partner, 'You go on. I'll be fine.' The other young Black Watch soldier went on alone until he reached the FUP (Forming Up Point). After a short while he asked the sergeant if he could go back to his friend,

> but he was abruptly told, 'No way! If you go back you'll be dead as well.'
>
> But the young soldier simply could not stop thinking of his friend lying out there, and remained insistent that he went. He persuaded the sergeant, who said, 'We'll be moving out of here in two hours, and if you're not back we'll consider you either missing or dead as well.'
>
> The soldier set off into the night and, just as the two hours were up, he was spotted carrying the body of his friend across a clearing and into the Forming Up Point. He laid his friend reverently on the ground. When the sergeant appeared he said, 'See, I told you he'd be dead. It wasn't worth your while.'
>
> The young Black Watch soldier stood up to his full height and, looking the much older sergeant squarely in the eye, said to him, 'He may be dead now, but he wasn't when I got to him. And just before he died, he said to me, "I knew you'd come, I knew you'd come."'

Each one of us might wish to be the kind of person who would act in this way, choosing an attitude of courage, loyalty and comradeship, rather than what might have seemed an easier course. What attitude do you take with you into the world each day? Is it the one you would like, or is it time to make changes and to choose a more positive approach?

A NEW WAY OF LOOKING AT THINGS

Many of the clients who come to me for coaching have powerful jobs, great influence, financial rewards and status. Yet they feel unhappy and dissatisfied. Many say they feel as though there is something missing in their lives. This is because they have neglected many of their own talents, beliefs and desires to the point where they don't even know what these might be. They have concentrated so hard on certain aspects of themselves and their lives that others have been lost.

My job is to help them rediscover the bigger picture, the things in themselves and their lives which make them feel whole, excited, creative and motivated. I aim to open up their choices for the future by encouraging them to explore their own talents and dreams. I try to help them develop a whole new way of looking at things, because no matter what we have achieved so far, whether it is a lot or a little, and no matter how young or old we are, there are still a wealth of possibilities to be explored and many, many options for future choices.

Do you know what you want? Have you made plans based on what is expected of you or predicted for you, or have you chosen what truly matters most to you? Take a long, hard look at yourself. What kind of person are you? What drives you? What is your idea of fun, of success, of satisfaction? Do you believe in yourself and have the courage to stand up for your beliefs? Do you trust your own judgement, and can you let people know where they stand with you? Do you choose goals which inspire you and which encourage you to push back frontiers?

The TICK Test

This test will help you to discover more about yourself and your abilities and is a great help when making plans and building dreams for the future. I use it for coaching clients, many of whom have told me that it has opened their eyes. Some have found it particularly useful when shared around a table with colleagues and with their families.

T Talents

Even the most high-powered people don't realise how many things they are good at. Make a list of all the talents you have, no matter how big or small, in every area of your life. Discovering just how many things you can do is the basis of confidence. It will open up all kinds of possibilities and move you out of the 'grey, work-obsessed' category and into the 'sparkling, interesting, open' one.

I Interests
List the interests you have, in as much detail as possible. What interests do you follow and which ones do you neglect? What would you love to spend more time doing? Do you spend time on things which have nothing to do with your job? Can you happily talk to a stranger at a party about something which interests you? What talents have you closed down, due to pressure of work or anxiety about success or failure?

C Challenges and choices
What do you want to do with the whole of your life? What kinds of choices have you made so far? What challenges excite and inspire you?

K Kindness
How kind are you towards yourself? Do you look after yourself, recognise what you need and provide it – for instance rest, a break, a change? Or are you tough, intolerant and demanding towards yourself? When someone gives you a compliment, do you accept it? Positive comments from others provide us with 'the wind beneath our wings', and should be valued.

When you have done the TICK test, look at the results you've come up with and see what stands out for you. Perhaps there is something you have always wanted to do, or a skill you would love to develop, or something you really enjoy but which you have had very little time for. Now is the time to start making these things a reality, to make them part of your future plans and then put those plans into action. Not only will you enjoy life more, but you will become a more fully rounded human being. The TICK test is all about finding a whole new way of looking at yourself and your future. What might you yet become and do? Anything you choose!

> The brilliant young financial director of a major bank was offered the opportunity to spend a year working in Australia. The idea was that, under the 'not for profit' sector of the company, he would set up a social responsibility wing and help others to launch businesses and social ventures. He jumped at such an exciting opportunity, but fully expected to return to his job in Britain afterwards. A year later he changed his mind. He loved the work he was doing and felt it was really worthwhile. He made the choice to stay on in Australia and create a new life for himself.

This man made a life choice which took him in a whole new direction. Not all of us switch continents as a result of our choices, but each one of us makes choices daily which affect the rest of our lives. Make sure the choices you make reflect who you really are, what you believe in and the direction you know is right for you.

NEW HORIZONS

If you have answered all three of the questions I posed at the beginning of this chapter, you will have taken the first big step towards opening up the horizons of your thinking and discovering many new possibilities for your life and work. Finding your own greatness begins with the courage to look inwards, with self-recognition and with real honesty.

chapter 2

Connecting the Heart to the Head

*T*oo many people work with their heads and ignore their hearts. The result is often success without joy, goals met with no true sense of achievement, and a working approach which can veer towards the demanding and bullying. This chapter is about making the connection between the head and the heart, between the thinking and the feeling aspects of oneself, in order to become a more fully rounded and effective human being.

People who rely almost exclusively on their left-brain – the logical, analytical, non-emotional side of the brain – are 'head' people. They rely on thought rather than feeling, and attempt to deal with any situation by being completely rational. Of course the ability to be logical and analytical is vital, and those who have it are often very successful. It is only when these left-brain abilities are relied on exclusively that problems arise.

There are many consequences of a totally left-brain approach. 'Head' people don't allow emotions, intuition, empathy and compassion to balance and enrich their logical skills, and the result is that they are disconnected from the human reactions and feelings of those they work with. This disconnection means that these people don't notice much of what is going on around them, or if they do notice they brush it aside because they have no idea how to deal with it. 'Head' people tend to work long hours, putting work ahead of many other aspects of their lives. They find it hard to see grey areas in work and in life: everything is either black or white.

Many organisations are run by 'head' people, and as a result those places are short on fun and flexibility and morale is often low. 'Head' people tend to run tough regimes, with no margin for error and no time for messing around.

> Max was a man who had all the trappings of success. He was managing director of a large finance company which he had helped to build from small beginnings. Max should have felt good about life: he had plenty of money, a large house and a lovely family. But he didn't feel good at all. He knew things were not right in his company. The profits were acceptable though not impressive, and more importantly, the staff looked miserable and the atmosphere was grim. This wasn't surprising, because Max wasn't a popular boss and he knew it. In fact many of his staff feared him and dreaded the regular criticisms he heaped on them. For some years Max had felt that his dictatorial style worked – people might fear him, but they got the job done. But of late he had begun to wonder if there might be another way to run things.

Max was clearly a man who operated from the head alone, and we shall come back to him shortly.

Of course, someone who operates purely from the heart, relying entirely on the right-brain approach of emotion, compassion, sympathy and empathy, will have a hard time too. It is impossible to be an effective manager if you are solely a 'heart' person. Discipline and boundaries fly out of the window and you may well be seen by those who work with you as gullible, over-soft and a pushover.

THE IDEAL BALANCE

What you should be aiming for is a blend of heart and head, a perfect balance of your logical skills with the empathy and compassion each one of us is capable of expressing. This is what it means to work from the inside out. And you can only achieve this balance once you have begun to know yourself.

Connecting the heart to the head leads to working with wisdom and generosity, sharing successes and creating a work environment in which people feel good and function well. When the heart and the head are in balance you save time and energy, improve performance and make effective decisions.

MAKING THE CONNECTION

No matter how disconnected the head and the heart may be, the connection between them can be made simply and quickly. The first step is to make bridges between the left and right sides of the brain. After that you can begin to look at decisions, events and patterns in your life from a connected point of view, and to choose to deal with them differently. This conscious effort will become automatic if you apply it consistently.

Exercise 1: Connecting the Left and Right Brains

Here is a simple exercise to help you connect the left (head) and right (heart) parts of the brain.

Sit quietly and close your eyes. Imagine a red rose in the right half of your brain. Now imagine a white rose in the left half of your brain. Next imagine these two roses being switched over, so that the red rose is in the left brain and the white rose is in the right brain.

This exercise has been found extremely effective, and as a result increases energy, creativity and relaxation. Repeat it every day for a few weeks. After that you can use it once every few days, or whenever you feel the connection needs reinforcing – for instance at a time of great stress.

Exercise 2: Extending the Connection

This exercise takes the connection between the head and the heart a step further.

Draw two circles, one labelled 'head' and the other 'heart'. Each of these circles represents an aspect of you. One may feel more developed and familiar than the other, but you have both capacities within you. Now draw a diagram in which the circles overlap slightly. This area of overlap is where the heart and the head connect. It is your true connection centre and the place from which you can choose to function most of the time.

Think of three decisions you have made recently. They might be work- or life-related, large or small. Which part of you, the head or the heart, took charge of each decision? How might the decision have changed if you had used the combined head-and-heart connection centre to make the decision?

> Geoff was the manager of a firm that sold fish, and one Friday he faced the miserable task of making four people redundant. The firm was in a small town where there were not many jobs going, and he knew that the people who would be losing their jobs that day had families to support. But Geoff was a man who operated from the head. His top-down manner

and style made him an issuer of instructions to the extent that his staff were often on edge and jumpy. One can only imagine how they must have felt on being summoned late on the Friday afternoon to his office. He told each person, briefly and without a flicker of emotion, that they had to go and didn't think about them again. A little later in the day a young trainee came up to Geoff and said sympathetically, 'Laying those people off must have been tough.' Geoff was startled – he hadn't thought of it as tough, simply as something that had to be done. He spent the weekend thinking about what the trainee had said, and about the people whose jobs had been lost. On the Monday morning Geoff went over to the trainee and said, 'I've been thinking and, you know, I could have handled things better on Friday.' He then phoned each of the people who had lost their jobs, asked them to come back and let him know how they were coping, and offered support. It took a nudge from someone else, but Geoff rediscovered his heart.

Geoff's initial reaction to dismissing those four people came from the head alone. He was disconnected from his employees' feelings and from his own, and the result of his dismissive style was deeply unhappy staff. Geoff obviously didn't feel too good about the way he had handled things, either. But he found the courage to rethink and to bring his heart into the picture. When he called the employees back and offered support he was acting from a balanced head-and-heart position.

As Geoff's story illustrates, bringing the heart into connection with the head doesn't necessarily change the decision – the four jobs still had to go. But it can change the way you handle a decision, leaving the people concerned knowing that you care and with their self-esteem intact.

Max, the MD I mentioned on p. 28, who had always relied on his head alone, came to see me because he felt so dissatisfied with the way things were going in his company. He arrived with his head down, and shoulders hunched, and barely acknowledged my assistant's greeting.

After Max had outlined his worries I asked him to do the head-and-heart connection exercises. He agreed, despite some scepticism. I also asked him to begin to review the way he was at work.

A few weeks later Max arrived at my office beaming and gave my assistant a warm hello before telling me that he had started to make changes, with amazing results. He had decided to notice what was going on with each member of his staff, and to respond to it using his heart as well as his head. When his assistant arrived looking unwell he had suggested she take the day off. When a young worker mentioned he had just become a dad, Max sent him a card and a bottle of champagne. When another employee messed up on a minor deal, instead of yelling at her Max invited her to discuss what had gone wrong and what she might do differently next time.

As Max changed the way he behaved, he noticed two things. Firstly, he began to enjoy the feeling that treating others well was giving him. And secondly, the atmosphere in the office was changing. More people were smiling and cheerful, and the gloom was lifting. 'I'd never have believed that by making simple changes to the way I do things I could make such a difference,' he told me.

Like Geoff, Max discovered that connecting his heart to his head was simple and very enjoyable. He liked the positive results he got: his own working life was improved, as well as that of his staff. As time went by Max was able to make more and more positive changes and his company became increasingly successful.

WORKING FROM THE CONNECTION CENTRE

When the head and the heart are well connected and working together, wonderful things happen. Bringing a little understanding and empathy to a tough situation often dissolves difficulties. In conflicts it becomes possible for everyone to walk away feeling like a winner. And when employees and colleagues feel you see them as people rather than just as functionaries, they respond by doing their jobs better. Here are ten of the positive results you can expect when you operate from your head-and-heart connection centre:

1. You are able to approach any situation by seeing the other person's point of view

Whether it's an adversary in a negotiation, someone who's messed up and is coming to see you for an appraisal, or simply a colleague asking for advice on a sensitive matter, you can put yourself in the other person's shoes. When you begin the exchange by understanding where they're coming from, it's likely to lead to a far more constructive outcome.

2. You can avoid conflict far more often

The person leading from the head-and-heart connection centre looks for a mediated solution to a problem, rather than heading straight for arbitration or even litigation. You will come to expect that conflicts can be resolved peacefully.

3. You will become aware of the way you are doing things

Like Geoff in the fish firm, you will still do what you have to do, but you will look at the way you're doing it and bring a degree of sensitivity to bear.

4. You will be flexible

When you approach a situation from the head-and-heart connection centre you are willing to listen to the opinions of others, to ask for and take advice, and to look for less obvious routes towards your goals.

5. There is more time for people

A person who has their head and heart connected notices the people around them and knows what's going on in the lives of people they work with. Taking a minute or so to say hello, to ask about a colleague's health/child/partner, to notice someone's appearance, makes all the difference. When you are connected you don't just work with people, you have relationships with them.

6. You learn to read the characters of those around you

Rather than appearing over-anxious to have your own way in everything, it is so much more effective to work with other people's strengths and potential. You will recognise what's happening and possible, rather than with what you think ought to happen.

7. You become a better communicator

The most important element of this is the ability to listen to others, not just with half an ear but fully. It will also help you to be consistent, which is a great asset. People who are nice one minute but nasty the next, and often unpredictable, are a nightmare to work with. This kind of behaviour comes from poor communication and bottling things up. Saying what you mean and meaning what you say, which is the connected position, will mean others know where they stand with you and they will come to value this consistency.

8. You are more easily able to admit to your own mistakes, flaws and frailties

So many 'head' people think they have to appear perfect in order to inspire respect or to succeed. This is far from the truth: each one of us gets things wrong and has weaknesses as well as strengths. To recognise yours and allow for them is wisdom.

9. You will have a far greater ability to help others reach their potential

Someone whose head and heart are connected is generous and enjoys seeing ability and enthusiasm in others. They have the time and energy to teach, to encourage and to inspire.

10. Your work/life balance will be right

If you come from either the head or heart alone it is very difficult to get the balance right – both types tend to work excessive hours. But the person whose head and heart are fully connected has the wisdom to know that too much is never a good thing. The managing director of a large corporation recently sent all the staff an email saying, 'I don't want to see you here after 6pm.' This was wise and generous, and gave his staff permission to enjoy their private lives to the full.

People who are operating from the head-and-heart connection centre take their time, even when the pressure is on. They are able to walk into a room at a calm, measured pace and to think before responding to others. They have a strong sense of who they are, and above all they are grounded.

Exercise: Grounding Yourself

'Head' people tend to be very ungrounded. The head is very heavy, and those who operate entirely from their heads tend to suffer from muscle tension in the head, neck, shoulders and back. When this happens, grounding yourself is vital. It is a simple and effective way of moving your power centre down from your head and releasing the pressure on your neck and shoulders.

Take a few moments to stand and feel the ground beneath your feet. Allow the ground to support you. Feel its strength and solidity. Feel the connection you have with the ground as it supports you. Now take a few deep breaths, while relaxing and lowering your shoulders. Imagine your centre of energy moving down from your head to your solar plexus.

This is a great exercise to do for a few moments before going into a meeting or facing any kind of high-pressure situation. You will arrive looking calm and centred, rather than tense and rushed.

MAKING THE MOST OF MEETINGS

Meetings are a fact of life in most organisations, and most of us go to more meetings than we would like. Many of the organisations I visit are overwhelmed with meetings, and yet most of the meetings don't achieve a lot. They are long, they are boring and many of them end with disappointment, frustration and plans for more meetings, rather than any really satisfying outcome.

When you are operating from the head-and-heart connection centre, however, you begin to see meetings in a different way. They are only valuable if they achieve something, and they need not take up too much of anyone's time. There are three key types of meeting which are effective and which, when used in combination, are often all that is needed for the effective running of any organisation.

1. The weekly meeting

This should be held first thing in the morning for no longer than twenty minutes. The key factor here is that everyone remains standing. This changes the dynamics of the meeting, puts everyone on an equal footing and produces amazing results. Often those who generally hold back will speak up in this kind of meeting, and it's great for generating ideas.

2. The monthly, formal meeting with a prepared agenda

This is a standard meeting which deals with routine business.

3. The one-to-one informal meeting

This is the one which makes all the difference. The boss walks into his or her employee's office, sits down and says,

'Tell me how I can help you to do your job better.' The person on the other side of the desk may be alarmed at first, but if these meetings become regular monthly events they will come to expect and appreciate them. It gives both sides a chance to be honest, to nip problems in the bud and to say what's on their minds. When two people working together connect in this way it becomes a building block in creating a more effective, productive relationship. If you really know what's going on for someone who works for you, it will prove valuable next time you face disaster or success. You will know what this person is made of, capable of and willing to do. Holding a regular meeting like this is equivalent to saying, 'I'm on your side and I want this to work.'

> A department head of a large legal firm told me that her staff were over-worked and demoralised. Their time was taken up with endless meetings and reports, and the atmosphere in the office was tense and unfriendly. No one had the time to say thank you, let alone pass the time of day or get to know one another better. I suggested she try cutting back the number of meetings and instigating the third type of meeting by dropping in on each of her staff for half an hour a week. A month later she told me that change was beginning to happen in the firm and everyone was respond-ing with enthusiasm. Her staff had been startled when she began the one-to-one meetings, but most of them loved having the chance to talk to her about their worries and plans. Already there was a warmer, brighter atmos-phere, people were smiling more and getting through the work faster because they felt they mattered.

HAVE A CORACLE IN YOUR BOARD ROOM

A few years ago I founded Columba 1400, a charity which helps people from all walks of life to achieve their potential and learn leadership skills. One of the most important things

I knew I wanted was to create an atmosphere in which everyone could have their say and be heard.

The charity, based on the beautiful Isle of Skye, is named after St Columba, who fled to Scotland from Ireland in AD 563 in a small round wood-and-bark boat called a coracle. He landed on the island of Iona, where he founded a monastery which became the cradle of Celtic Christianity in Scotland. When we began fund-raising in 1997 for the charity I had decided to name after this remarkable man, it was exactly 1400 years since his death. We decided to have a coracle-shaped table in the board room, and this was one of the first things we put in place.

When a new group of young people or visitors comes to the centre we eat dinner round this table, then introduce our visitors to a 'coracle conversation'. This is rather in the manner of the Native American talking stick which when held gives that person the right to speak and to the devoted attention of the assembled 'coracle'. Go round the table and each person in turn, if they so wish, speaks about something important to them. It may be about an event which has inspired them or touched them that day, something which is holding them up in their lives, or simply a little story they would like to tell everyone else. It is not so much desperate unloading as simply opening up a little in a warm and inviting atmosphere.

Recently a group of academics from the United States came to visit us, and they told us the coracle had been the most significant moment of their trip. These learned men were used to business dinners and to defending their corner, which left them feeling weary and uninspired. They told us that after our coracle dinner they felt they had been able to give something and had gained a great deal. They left the table feeling much better for the experience.

This is an idea that any organisation can use and adapt.

Sitting around a table, especially if you have just eaten together, creates an atmosphere in which it is possible to be more open and to talk and listen to one another.

If each person puts forward one idea, one thing they have learned that day or one suggestion, the whole organisation will benefit. The ultimate aim is that every person should leave a coracle feeling uplifted, and that they have both given and gained.

> The chief executive of Columba 1400 is a young Canadian, Ian Chisholm, who arrived at the centre like a breath of fresh air. He is a fine example of someone whose heart and head are connected. Whenever there is a problem he will say, 'Let's put it out there – let's put everything on the table, talk about it and sort it out.' This straightforward, simple and effective approach has left many 'head' people catching their breath. It not only works, but it helps other people to begin connecting their hearts to their heads.

DEVELOP PEOPLE SKILLS

Networking is one of the buzz words of the moment, a term which encompasses meeting and talking to as many others as you can in order to make useful contacts and advance your business interests. But to me, networking is an arid, overused and soulless term for an activity in which people seldom make satisfying or genuine connections. However, when your head and heart are connected you become more interested in developing people skills. By this I mean taking a real interest in others, talking to them about themselves or about subjects of mutual interest and making enjoyable connections, while keeping your business cards in your pocket.

If you like other people and enjoy expanding your circle of friends and acquaintances, good business contacts will follow. Think about people first and business second and you will be successful. If your job becomes your identity, you become one-dimensional and dull and people won't be drawn to you.

Many highly successful people don't make good connections with others simply because they are nervous and lack confidence in social situations.

> I once coached a bright young government minister who confessed that he dreaded any kind of public function because he inevitably ended up stuck in a corner talking to someone boring. When we looked at how this happened he explained that he felt very anxious when faced with a function at which he was expected to appear. He would walk into the room too fast, head down, and make straight for anyone who looked available to talk to. With practice this minister learned to take his time, walk in slowly, smiling and looking confident, speak to the staff who were serving drinks, which is extremely important, and wait calmly for people to come up to him. That way he was able to choose who to talk to and to feel in control of the situation. A few weeks later he reported that his fear of social situations was disappearing and he was beginning to enjoy the busy round of ministerial social engagements.

When you feel calm and in control it is easier to take a genuine interest in others. Nerves and anxiety can prevent you from listening well, and get in the way of a good exchange. Being a people person is a true sign of having a strong head-and-heart connection. It is something you can cultivate and practise over time, and it is well worth the effort.

To develop people skills, remember these points:

1. Walk slowly
Even if it feels odd at first, slow down, never rush, and look up and not down as you enter a room.

2. Smile warmly

Keep an open, warm expression as much as possible. Smiling is hugely effective in attracting others to you.

3. Ask questions

Talk to other people about themselves and what they do. Never rush to tell them all about yourself.

4. Hold business back

That includes your cards and details of your job. Save them for the right moment, further down the line.

5. Keep in touch

A thank you note, an invitation to a drink or lunch, a congratulatory card or just a friendly call are all great ways to follow up when you meet someone interesting.

> One of the best modern communicators I know is John Milligan, a man who began as a miner and worked his way up until he was the head of a vast company supplying oil rigs. He is now a millionaire with a fabulous country estate. Despite his great wealth, John has never become arrogant or stopped being concerned about others. He once arrived at a smart country club where he was sponsoring a golf tournament. As he went up the steps he stopped to talk to the doorman and asked him whether he had had any lunch. When the doorman said no, John immediately made arrangements for him to get some, throwing the organisation of the event into disarray in the process. This act of kindness and concern is typical – he is a man who makes friends in all walks of life. He would always say that his biggest and best business deals were those with people whose friendship he had cultivated over many years. He kept in touch with people he had met, was genuinely interested in them and would wait, perfectly relaxed, for the right moment to do a deal.

STAY CONNECTED

Once you experience the rewards and results of connecting your heart to your head, you will want to stay connected. And like any other habit in life, this will happen when you practise it consistently. Moments of stress are the times when you are most likely to revert to 'head' behaviour, so these are the times when you need to pause for a few moments and ask yourself the following questions:

1. Am I taking my own time, no matter what pressure there is to be speedy?
2. Do I need to step out of the situation for a few minutes, just to feel the air on my face, breathe deeply and ground myself?
3. Am I treating others around me fairly and considerately?

Remember that any moment of stress is just that, a moment, which will pass and be forgotten. Keep your head and heart connected and you won't lose your cool, do something you will later regret or make a bad judgement. When your head and heart are connected you are solid and sound, you know yourself, you know why you are doing what you are doing and you know where you are going.

chapter 3

Look
After
Yourself

*t*There are plenty of people who have won success at a high price. We all know examples of the executive with an ever-expanding girth, the pencil-thin sharp dresser who has become an exercise junkie, the ladder-climbing young trainee who keeps going with stimulant drugs, or the company boss who likes a tipple or six after work. We know them because they exist in virtually every major company in the Western world, and in many smaller ones too.

What all these people are doing is functioning, rather than living. They have found ways to cope with the demands of their lives, ways to push themselves beyond reasonable limits and keep themselves going long after they need to stop. They are turning to addictions such as food, exercise, drugs, alcohol or work to cope with a life which feels overwhelming and hugely stressful. What they are doing is choosing avoidance. The coping strategies they have opted for help them to blank out the real issue they need to face. This issue is the one most of us need to address – self-care.

These people, and the many thousands just like them, have no real idea how to take care of themselves or what it means to balance the mind, body and soul and to feel physically and mentally in great shape. In the corporate world, lack of self-care is the norm. In many workplaces it is considered appropriate, even essential, to drive yourself on at a break-neck pace. The result is a large portion of the workforce which is '*beschränkt und erschöpft*'. This apt German phrase means to be hemmed in and limited (*beschränkt*) and exhausted (*erschöpft*). Are you '*beschränkt und erschöpft*'? Are you pushing yourself beyond reasonable limits, ignoring the warning signals your body might be giving you and dismissing self-care as unnecessary?

WHAT IS SELF-CARE?

Many people equate self-care with self-indulgence, seeing it as a luxury they can manage without. They couldn't be more wrong. Self-care is vital and appropriate; without it we risk mental, emotional and physical problems which can affect the way we function in all areas, and may ultimately even shorten our lives.

Self-care is about self-respect and self-worth. If you value yourself and the contribution you have to make, then you will be willing to make the effort involved in looking after yourself. To look after yourself requires self-discipline and a mental decision that you need not be lethargic or unfit. This includes all the basics – eating healthily, getting exercise and having enough sleep. It includes avoiding any kind of dependence on stimulants and any kind of addictive behaviour. It also means taking a long, hard look at your life and finding the right balance between your home life and your work life, even if this means making adjustments.

There is nothing clever about neglect. Yet hundreds of thousands of people neglect themselves on a long-term basis. I hope you will choose not to be among them. Knowing yourself from the inside out means looking after yourself. And looking after yourself is a habit you can cultivate and come to enjoy. In fact when you get used to looking after yourself you will wonder how so many people can fail to. Just like anything else, if you stick at it for long enough it becomes a way of life. A way of life worth having and worth living.

Success at the cost of your health and wellbeing has little value. True success incorporates a feeling of physical and mental wellbeing and it is the only success worth having.

> I once sat in on a board meeting of a major British company. Around the table were five men and three women and, as I came to realise, every one of them had a major health problem. One had just had a heart bypass operation and was still taking large amounts of medication. Another had a hidden alcohol problem. A third was seriously overweight, while a fourth suffered from periods of serious depression and was on long-term anti-depressants. Of the remaining four one was a chain smoker, one of the women appeared painfully thin, one was in remission from cancer and the last suffered from insomnia and could not get to sleep at night without sleeping pills. Yet these eight people were making decisions which affected the lives of many thousands of others.

Unusual? I don't think so. Such stresses and anxieties, and their effects, are not uncommon. These were good people, dedicated, skilled and hard-working. Yet all of them seemed utterly unable to look after themselves.

I had been asked to coach one of them, a charming and able man who turned out to be an insomniac. When I asked him to tell me about the ways in which he looked after his health he looked at me blankly and then mentioned membership of an exclusive gym, which he had managed to visit three times in as many months.

Over the next few weeks he and I put together a health plan for him to follow. Nothing too strenuous or demanding, just subtle shifts in the way he led his life. He began to take a little regular exercise, to eat more healthily and to spend less time in the office. He allowed himself more pleasures: he loved the cinema and began to see more films; he enjoyed walking in the open air, and now did this whenever he could; and he spent more time with his wife and two daughters.

Three months later he appeared again, looking much fitter, and told me that he had been able to throw away his sleeping pills. For the first time in years he could make decisions without having his mind clouded by exhaustion, and he felt good. What this man did, anyone can do. Learning to look after yourself is like giving your life an injection of fresh energy and enthusiasm. Who wouldn't choose to do that?

Do You Need to Look After Yourself?

Answer yes or no to the following questions.

- Do you feel tired when you get to work most days?
- Do you rely on something external to get you through the day? (This may include anything from an excess of coffee to sugar, alcohol or drugs)
- Do you take little or no exercise?
- Do you regularly feel irritable or depressed?
- Are you under- or overweight?
- Do you regularly stay at work for more than ten hours a day?
- Are you always rushing?
- Do you often feel alone and without real support?
- Do you often rely on fast food?
- Would you change anything major in your life if you could?

If you answered yes to any of these questions, it's time to pause for thought. If you answered yes to three or more of the questions, it's time to begin looking after yourself.

CHOOSE GOOD HEALTH

Looking after yourself also means looking after your health. Working yourself into the ground, racing around all day and ignoring niggling aches and pains can lead to long-term health problems. Stress illnesses are epidemic in the West. Too many people are not living long enough to enjoy their retirement. Looking after your health need not be a chore or add still more to your 'to do' list. If you approach it in that way it won't be very effective anyway. Instead, think of it as a bonus and a gift, the chance to feel truly well, to enjoy getting up each day, knowing that you have good health and lots of energy, all in return for a little self-discipline and a few shifts of perspective.

Eight Simple ways to Look After Your Health

1. Eat well

If you don't put the correct fuel into a car, it won't go. And if you don't fuel your body with the right nutrients, it will lack energy and become ill. The rules of eating well are very simple:

- Eat enough but not too much
- Avoid junk foods, fast foods and sugar
- Eat plenty of fruit and vegetables
- Cut back on red meat, alcohol and coffee
- Drink plenty of water. Recent studies have proven that children function better and learn better if they drink plenty of water. This is true for adults too.

2. Take exercise

Without exercise our bodies seize up and become, stiff, creaky and tense. Exercise is a wonderful release and leaves us feeling better. Choose any exercise which appeals to you and do it regularly. Walking is as good as anything else, as long as you walk briskly and for at least half an hour three or four times a week.

3. Get enough sleep

Sleep is a vastly under-rated health benefit which is available to all of us. When was the last time you monitored your own sleep pattern and, instead of pushing through the sleep/pain barrier, allowed yourself to relax properly? By granting ourselves the gift of a couple of good nights' sleep in succession, perhaps over a weekend, we can achieve measurable differences in temperament, outlook and output.

It was only recently that I discovered the benefits of twenty minutes spent relaxing in a hot muscle-soak bath, followed by a cup of sleep-inducing chamomile tea and an early night. Why not try it yourself?

4. Enjoy the extras

The word 'extra' appeals to me far more than 'alternative' when it comes to the benefits of health care above and beyond the purely conventional. Many of us might feel a little shy about such treatment, but it is well worth overcoming your reservations. Before a visit to the United States which was packed with commitments, I found to my consternation that my wife had booked me in for an aromatherapy massage. It turned out to be destressing and detoxifying bliss, and I was grateful to her for pushing me towards such a valuable and worthwhile 'extra'. There are many similar extra forms of health therapy available, and it is well worth considering any which might help you to relax, stay in good health and increase your sense of wellbeing.

5. Pace yourself

Hurtling through life at incredible speed is damaging to your health. Eventually this kind of pace proves impossible to maintain – your body will refuse to continue, and you will become ill or collapse. Living on adrenalin is bad for you, yet many people do it. Adrenalin is the fight-or-flight hormone which is produced at times of high stress. When it is regularly produced it takes a great toll on your body, and in particular the liver.

Learning to slow down and pace yourself at a speed which feels comfortable and right, is a challenge worth facing. Begin to look at ways of pacing yourself a little more gently and of using your time to benefit yourself as well as others. For instance, you could take a break between appointments instead of racing straight back to the 'to do' list.

> Father Dominic Milroy, the distinguished former headmaster of one of England's most famous Catholic schools, Ampleforth College in Yorkshire, was regularly asked to speak at conferences and other events around the country. He always said that he would 'never return to Ampleforth on the same day as that when he had been speaking elsewhere'. His mind, body and spirit needed time to recover and renew, ready for the tasks which faced him on his return.

Do you know what kind of recovery time you need after facing a demanding engagement or commitment? Knowing yourself involves knowing what you need in order to perform at your best.

One of the most useful things I learned from watching others was to take a break with a good novel when on a plane journey, rather than spending the whole time ploughing through business papers. Perhaps this is the sign of a really successful, balanced executive.

6. *Accept support*

Too often we feel that, in life and in work, choices, changes and decisions are things we have to manage alone. The closer you are to the top of the corporate ladder, the less likely you are to turn to others for support or guidance. Many chief executives feel that, as the deciding voice, they should not be seen to depend on or resort to contributions from others.

Yet a guiding voice, a wise suggestion, a nudge in the right direction can be of immense value. This is often why clients come to me for coaching. Many of them, despite their success, feel quite isolated and without support. Making the decision to choose a source of support, be it coaching or any other appropriate avenue, is an act of generosity to yourself.

In the same way, the help of a personal fitness trainer can be very supportive and can make the difference between the success or failure of a resolution to get fit. In my own case meeting 'Dan the Man' at my youngest son's swimming lessons was of huge benefit. Gently and with humour he has prodded and cajoled me into getting into shape and eating more healthily, managing to make the whole experience more of a pleasure and less of an ordeal.

7. *Be true to yourself*

By this I mean find the courage to use your own judgement, no matter what others think or what pressure you come under. Make choices which fit in with your personal belief system and stay consistent. If you don't you will find it hard to honour yourself, and if you don't honour yourself you will not be mentally and emotionally healthy. Take a little time, especially when faced with complex questions, to decide what your belief system is and what your personal views are. I say this because many people, even those of advanced years, are still taking on the beliefs of others as their own. Be aware of your own views first, and then be prepared to synchronise them with the views of others, accepting the differences and finding common ground where it exists.

8. Have fun

Laughter brings the most immeasurable health benefits. It greatly increases our feelings of wellbeing, and its healing powers have been well researched and documented. Children laugh many times a day, yet as adults we may not laugh for days on end. Even a smile is of huge value, causing the release of all kinds of beneficial chemicals in the brain and instantly lifting the spirits of those who witness it, as well as of the person who is smiling. Try smiling more often. Look for reasons to laugh. If you have children, join in with their laughter. Life is a serious business, but we should always take it lightly.

> Jane was a high-flying executive who managed to juggle her demanding job in a textiles company with being a wife and the mother of two young children. When she came to see me she was managing to keep all the balls in the air but was running on empty, exhausted and in danger of making herself ill. Jane, as she realised when we began to talk, was looking after everyone but herself. She feared she would have to give up her job.
>
> However, a little careful planning thought up by the two of us went a long way. She stopped taking her children to a day nursery and invested in a really good nanny, which gave her more peace of mind, more support and more flexibility with her time. Jane had been living on sandwiches grabbed between meetings and had also been doing paperwork late into the night after the children were in bed. She began to eat more healthily and agreed to my suggestion that she stop doing office work at home for two months. She also booked herself a weekly massage and a long weekend away with her husband. Two months later Jane told me her energy and outlook had improved beyond all recognition.

THE WORK/LIFE BALANCE

Getting the balance right between your life in the workplace and your life beyond it is the critical mainstay of looking after yourself. This balance is more important than any other single aspect of self-care.

Far too many people feel they have to put in excessive hours at work. In the developed world we have moved into a culture in which people are proud of working long hours and feel that doing so demonstrates some kind of virtue, despite the miserable consequences on their lives. When you work excessive hours your relationships with partners, children and friends have no time or space to flourish, and in fact they often suffer. You have no time for other interests and are likely to appear single-minded and dull. You begin to overidentify with your work and to see yourself in terms of what you do rather than who you are. There are two dangers here: not only will you become boring, but if you lose your job you will lose your sense of self too.

No job worth having demands excessive hours. Doing your job well involves doing it in an appropriate number of hours per day. Of course there may be odd days when you need to work for longer, but this should not occur on a daily basis.

If you feel obliged to work excessively long hours, ask yourself why. Where does the pressure come from? Is it self-imposed? Is it the company ethos? A demanding boss? Or is the company short-staffed? Whatever the reason, once you have identified it you can begin to address it and decide how to shift the balance.

Think it can't be done? This is never true. If you want to make changes, you can. You may need to go slowly, to make those changes subtly rather than dramatically, but the principle of change is always possible.

If you are reluctant to create a healthier work/life balance, it is useful to consider why. Might working fewer hours bring you up against something you have been avoiding, such as the lack of a partner in your personal life, or an unhappy existing relationship? When we make shifts, the arid and needy areas of our life are often exposed and we become painfully aware of them. It can be shocking to recognise that you have been ignoring or avoiding a part of your life which needs nurture and attention. But exposing the situation more clearly is a good thing: it will give you a chance to begin to put it right.

Remember, too, that the healthier and more balanced you are the more easily you will manage your job and the demands of the workplace. Working excessive hours is a self-perpetuating cycle – the more hours you do the more hours you need to do. Say no, now!

Sarah was ambitious and determined, and when she joined a large merchant bank she worked her way steadily up the career ladder to a very senior position. Dedicated, and very conscious of her position as a woman in a world dominated by men, she never took a day off sick and worked extremely long hours, often not arriving home until ten at night. By the age of thirty-eight Sarah had achieved a great deal at work, but her private life was like a parched desert. She had few close friends, lived alone and had not had a boyfriend for three years. It was only when she began to review her life and to look at the balance that Sarah realised something had to change. Over the next six months she began to cut back her hours, and discovered that she could leave the office at six most days and still do a good job. What is more, her boss told her he was relieved to see she wasn't staying so late. Sarah put the energy she was saving at work into developing her social life, and eventually met someone she wanted to marry.

Exercise: Are You Firing on All Cylinders?

This is an exercise I often give my clients to help them identify areas where their lives may be out of balance. To function at your absolute best you need to keep your life in balance,
and this means firing equally strongly on all six 'cylinders'. If
one or two of them are down it will affect all the others.

The first three cylinders are work-related, and I find that
with most clients these areas are fine. The last three relate
to life outside work and your life as a whole, and it is usually
in one or more of these areas that my clients find they are
a cylinder or two down as their personal lives take second
place to their working lives.

However, all six are equally important. Firing on all cylinders is about living your life in balance. If you aren't firing
on all six cylinders, the 'engine' that is your life can't spark
into action and be fully firing and ready for action. With
just one cylinder down it cannot rev into full throttle and
will sound a little tired and damp. Take a little time now to
look at the cylinders and ask yourself if each of them is fully
active in your life.

Strategy (awareness)

This concerns your ability to stand back from your life, or
from a given situation, and see the bigger picture with insight
and good judgement. You are aware of your role, you are
able to plan ahead and you recognise opportunities as they
arise.

Decision-making (focus)

In this area of life you cultivate the vital ability to discrim-
inate between what is important and what is not, and to
make decisions with wisdom and balance.

Other interests (creativity)

Do you make space in your life for creativity and for interests which are not related to your work? Do you dance, paint, sing, play sports, hike up mountains or do whatever else sets your spirit free?

Personality (integrity)
Do others trust you and know where they stand with you? Do you know yourself well and know when to hold back and when to step in? This area of life includes your personal relationships with partner, family, children and friends.

Administration (perseverance)
This includes your personal administration, time management, discipline and ability to manage the many agendas of your life with smooth efficiency.

Humanity (service)
This covers your connection to the wider world. Do you contribute to your area and your community? Do you help those who are in need? This area includes your compassion and your ability to give without expectation of receiving.

Time to Reflect

Working out where you are firing well and where you are running out of steam or simply not confident is the first step. The next is to begin redressing the balance. When you discover, as so many of us do, that you are a cylinder or two down and that some areas of your life are being neglected, how do you begin to change things and get the missing cylinders firing?

Sometimes clients in this position want to leap into action, coming up with lists, plans and models for altering their lives. But I always suggest that they will benefit far more by doing the opposite. Nothing is more valuable, at this stage, than taking a little time out to reflect, review and refocus. I firmly believe that it is only by 'chilling and stilling' – chilling out and stilling the mind – that you can find the mental space and energy needed to address the rebalancing of your life. So rather than rushing to do something, take a little time out to simply be and to allow fresh impetus and recognition to surface.

Rudi Giuliani, the highly successful Mayor of New York at the time of the 11 September 2001 Twin Towers tragedy, always said that at the toughest moments in his life he would take time out to sit quietly, perhaps have a neck and shoulder massage, and reflect on his next step. Winston Churchill offers another marvellous example of the value of time to reflect and review. When he found himself out of office in the 1930s, he headed off to his country residence where he escaped from the world and spent his time building a wall, brick by brick. At that time he had no idea he would be called to prominence in British history during the Second World War, but when it happened he was ready, having taken time out to review his life and to recharge his energy.

> Ian was the chief executive officer of a multinational company and he came to see me at a time when he felt seriously stressed. He did the cylinders test and was disconcerted to find that, while his three work cylinders were fine and his family relationships were strong, his humanity and interests cylinders were all down. Ian took some time to think about how this had happened and what changes he might like to make to redress the balance in his life. When we met again he told me, with great enthusiasm, that he had once been a keen runner and had also enjoyed amateur jazz singing. He decided to take up these activities again and set himself the challenge of running a half-marathon. He also decided to spend a couple of hours each week helping to run a local children's football team. With all six cylinders firing strongly Ian felt happier and more relaxed, and was more productive at work.

THE TROUBLE WITH ANXIETY

Anxiety is the modern plague. Debilitating and destructive, it can undermine your health and happiness in a major way if you allow it to. You cannot look after yourself properly or live your life in balance if you are dominated by anxiety. Many of the clients I see have marvellous lives, but they don't see it that way. The permanent black cloud of anxiety beneath which they live obliterates many of the good things in their lives.

What are they anxious about? Anything and everything. We've all got reasons to be anxious. Will that deal come off? Will I keep my job? Will I get a pension? How can I cope with money troubles? Will my marriage survive? Will the children's problems be solved?

If you are prone to anxiety it can be tough to break the cycle. The following simple techniques may help.

Focus on Success

People who don't suffer from anxiety do this naturally, but it can also be learned. When worries and problems enter your mind simply refuse to focus on them. Instead, choose a more positive and appealing thought that gives you a sense of pleasure, success or optimism. For instance, you might replace the thought. 'Will the deal come off?' with 'The last deal was great and this one will be too.' When you run a particular anxiety round and round in your mind it inevitably grows bigger and darker. The same is true of a pleasant thought – it can be very powerful, changing the way you feel and influencing your entire day.

Take a Detox Moment

This is a marvellous thing to do regularly, perhaps at the beginning and end of each day. Enable your mind to clear itself of all thoughts by relaxing to some beautiful music for a few minutes, looking at a stunning view or simply listening to the silence. This kind of mental 'detox' can produce marvellous results. If the mind is allowed to clear itself and rest, new ideas and fresh energy will result. In *Lonesome Dove*, author Larry McMurtry describes the way Captain Woodrow Call takes moments like this: 'It was something he had always done – moved apart, so he could be alone and think things out a little . . . often in a tight situation his mind would seem to grow tired from so much hard thinking. He would sink for a time into a blankness, only to come out of it in the midst of an action he had not planned.'

Know When It's Worth Worrying

Here is a great story which illustrates this point very well. Marmaduke Hussey, who was then managing director of *The Times*, and later Chairman of the BBC, once said to his good friend Alec Douglas-Home, who was then Prime Minister: 'How on earth do you manage, with so many worries to address?' To which Alec replied: 'I only ever worry about the things I can influence.' There is great wisdom and great release in choosing not to worry when you simply can't change or influence a situation. Begin by recognising the difference between those things you can change and those you can't.

A client of mine admitted during our second session together that anxiety was ruining his life. He worried so much that it had simply become a habit, and as soon as one worry proved unnecessary he would find another to take its place. I encouraged him to take a detox moment at the beginning and end of each day, and to focus on good things instead of on his worries. This took some practice, but after a few weeks he told me he was feeling a great deal more confident and happy. As these changes became more habitual he began to look around for good things to focus on, in the same way that he had once looked around for worries. He told me: 'The funny thing is that when problems do come along I cope with them more effectively now that I'm not constantly dwelling on them.'

KNOW WHEN TO STOP

Having your life in balance and looking after yourself well gives you the wisdom to know the difference between enough and too much. Many people simply don't know when to stop, which can cause all kinds of problems. It can mean the difference between striking a good financial deal and a great one. It can mean the difference between a speech which bores the pants off everyone and a speech which inspires. And it can mean the difference between keeping your cool and losing your temper.

We live in an 'I want it and I want it now' society. But the wise person knows that the right moment to make a move may not be the present moment. Stopping a meeting at a good point and scheduling another meeting may be far more effective than drawing the meeting out until everyone is exhausted in order to push the deal through quickly.

Every one of us has an 'enough' level, and if we're pushed beyond it we feel overwhelmed. This leads to stress, exhaustion and anger, which may implode in a pounding headache or explode in an outburst of temper.

ENCOURAGE YOURSELF

Looking after yourself means appreciating and encouraging yourself. After all, if you don't appreciate your talents, efforts and achievements how can you feel good about yourself? And if you don't feel good about yourself you are not likely to be enjoying your life to the full or looking after yourself in the way that you deserve.

When clients first come to me they are often deflated or discouraged about some aspect of their work or lives. When I see someone in this state I ask them to run through with me the many achievements, gifts and blessings that they have. Although often reluctant to begin this exercise, most people enjoy it once they get going, describing to me good things in their lives which they had forgotten, dismissed or put to one side. Very often they tell me afterwards that hearing the list of their blessings and achievements has reminded them that they have plenty to live for and go for. It has given them a lift, encouraging them to go forward into a brave new tomorrow. Encouraging yourself is not self-congratulatory or indulgent. It is an appropriate and effective way of lifting your spirits and seeing things in perspective.

I once coached a man who was extraordinarily hard on himself and, as a result, on others around him. He was an actuary, a man who calculates insurance risks, and was extremely clever but not well liked at the firm where he worked. He was one of those people who always had to be right – he was exact and precise and allowed no margin for error. If anyone brought him an idea or a project he would immediately criticise it and point out the pitfalls or potential problems.

We spent some time looking at this. He recognised that his father had been very tough on him, and that his own behaviour was actually a search for recognition and acceptance. When I asked him to run through his achievements and qualities he was surprised and a little unsure, but he soon came to see just how much he had to be proud of. By encouraging himself in this way he gained a level of self-acceptance which changed his outlook.

His next step was to try doing something at which he was prepared to fail, so he took up the age-old Scottish sport of curling. Through this new activity he not only learned to lose with grace, but made new friends who valued him as a good companion and a team player. The result was a softer, more generous approach at work. He became someone to whom others could go for advice and reassurance – a remarkable turnaround.

EXPLORE YOUR SPIRITUAL SIDE

While looking after your physical health it is also important to develop and explore your spiritual side. As human beings we are capable of great depths of enlightenment and understanding, and if we don't explore these possibilities in ourselves we miss out on a deep sense of satisfaction and peace. The belief that there's a purpose and meaning to life, that it is a whole of which we are just a part and an energy or power which will support us through times of need, is vital if we are to become fully developed as human beings. There is a sense of fulfilment and completeness which comes with finding spiritual understanding, in whatever form it arrives, which is enriching and profound and which lifts us beyond the mundane and the day-to-day.

Many people choose to bypass this area, setting it aside as the practical and material demands of life take over. But developing your spiritual side – and we all have one – is very simple and can only support and enhance a busy, outgoing lifestyle. Without this spiritual dimension we are flat, lacking real purpose, and life is arid.

There are many paths that those who are interested in spirituality can take, but they all lead towards a sense of personal peace and fulfilment. St Ambrose of Milan said: 'Begin the work of peace within yourself so that once you are at peace yourself you can bring peace to others.' How you find your personal peace is for you to explore and discover. It is a matter of learning how and where your soul is at one with your circumstances and surroundings. It may lie in a glorious sunset, a walk along a beautiful beach or time spent in a place where you have known happiness and love. It may be found through the route of worshipping in an established church, or through a private spiritual discipline or practice such as meditation.

61

If you are prepared to discipline yourself mentally and physically, the journey of spiritual discipline will be even more challenging and exciting. Indeed, beginning your personal spiritual journey is a fundamental part of discovering who you are, why you are doing what you are doing, and what you want to do with the rest of your life. Developing your spiritual side will bring you to greater heights of peace and understanding, health and ease. It will allow you to forgive yourself for past mistakes, to understand your journey through life and to maintain balance, no matter what rocks you.

Exercise: Take the ACE Test

This is a very simple but extremely useful little test that you can apply to obtain an instant review of your life. It takes a couple of minutes, but will tell you a great deal. Ask yourself how much of you is given to each of the following sections of your life:

- Achievement
- Contribution
- Enjoyment

If you give yourself in equal measure to all three areas, your life is in a good state of balance. If one area is lacking, for instance if you achieve a great deal and contribute a great deal but have very little enjoyment, then recognising this will help you begin to redress the balance. And balance, when you achieve it, is everything.

chapter 4

Bring Your Home Self to Work

Many people lead a double life, as one person at work and another at home. Does this sound a little strange? Let me explain. I often find that the person who is a warm, loving partner and parent at home walks through the office doors in the morning and transforms into a tough, abrasive dictator. The person who is caring, sharing and relaxed at the kitchen table becomes tense, rigid and critical when the table is in the board room.

In this chapter I want to explain the importance of bringing your home self to work – that is, of being a fully rounded, thinking, feeling and perceptive human being in all situations, not just in your personal life. If people at home and people at work see you in quite different ways, that is because you are dividing yourself and leaving at home vital characteristics which might enhance and enrich your working life.

63

the Spirit of Success

I believe it is important for us to be ourselves, with all our attributes, flaws and characteristics, wherever we are and whatever the setting.

The ability to separate off parts of your personality when at work was summed up for me by the husband of a senior civil servant whom I was coaching. This very talented woman was having trouble motivating her team and I was brought in to give her some support. After a few private meetings I spent a day shadowing her in various office meetings and briefings. As part of this day we had arranged to have lunch with her husband, who worked from home and took a major role in the care of their two children. As we talked about the issues upon which we needed to concentrate the husband leaned back in his chair and said to me, 'You've got her right, but there's one thing you don't know – she never takes her home personality to work.'

He went on to explain that the loving mum who dropped the children off at school in the morning would tighten inwardly as she approached work, to the point that she became an entirely different person. The woman who loved singing, teaching in Sunday school and cycling with her family would become, in the time it takes to go through a revolving door, a hard-edged, hard-driven woman with no time at all for personal touches.

This was borne out when she and I returned to the office. While she took a high-level phone call I chatted to a researcher in her department, Anne, who told me of her delight that her third daughter had just graduated from the third of Glasgow's universities, Glasgow Caledonian. Since her first daughter had graduated from the first, Glasgow, and her second daughter from the second, Strathclyde, this was rather a unique hat-trick. When I returned to my client's office I mentioned Anne's delight at her daughters' achievements, to which my client replied, 'And which is Anne?'

This lack of connection with a significant member of her department was an indication of the extreme pressure and tension my client felt at work. At home, as the far more relaxed mother, wife and singer, she would have known this background information about someone she saw every day. Yet like so many executives, and others at every level of the work arena, she kept whole areas of her personality separate from work and private from her colleagues.

FEARS AND FALLACIES

The reason why so many people behave in such different ways at home and at work is fear. They don't want to let down their guard, appear vulnerable, wet or a target. They somehow imagine that if they open up, share information about themselves, relax a little and soften their attitude they will find a knife in their backs. By staying rigid and holding themselves back, they imagine they are doing a good job and protecting themselves.

In fact the opposite is true. The more unbending and rigid you are at work, the more you transform into a one-dimensional personality and the less you will be appreciated, successful or liked. Whereas when you take your home personality to work you become more human, more interesting, better able to cope with the pace and more effective at your job.

On a residential leadership course I ran for a government agency I asked everyone to take part in an exercise which involved exchanging personal information. It was only when they did this that two female executives who had worked side by side for years discovered that they shared a love of ballet. Even more striking, two male members of the board found that they supported the same football team and sat in the home supporters' stand every Saturday without knowing that the other was there. Out of this pooled information new friendships and bonds were formed. Soon after this course the team faced a tough time, with public buffetings and political shenanigans. The team were able to stand as one and to withstand these difficulties, strengthened by the new bonds they had formed.

65

In her wonderful song 'The Rose', the singer and actress Bette Midler sums up the price you pay for being afraid to be your whole self:

> *It's the heart afraid of breaking that never learns to*
> *dance,*
> *It's the dream afraid of waking that never takes the*
> *chance,*
> *It's the one who won't be taken who cannot seem to*
> *give,*
> *And the soul afraid of dying that never learns to live.*

It is also often the case that people believe keeping their home and work lives separate is the correct thing to do. They feel that talking about their home lives is out of bounds, and as a result they often appear to be very dry, one-sided individuals.

> A young Australian banker had always come across to his colleagues as a dull, lifeless sort who was rather uncertain of himself. He was so careful never to talk of his personal life that they concluded he must be just as dull away from the office as he was in it.
>
> This young banker attended a development seminar I was holding in his company, and in the break several of us began to chat about our lives. At this point the young banker revealed that he had children aged one and two and that his wife was expecting a third. His face lit up when he spoke of his family and he became a totally different person, passionate, warm and loving. Astonished, one of his colleagues said, 'I never knew you were a father.' The young banker replied that he had thought he wasn't supposed to talk about his private life at work, since no one had ever asked him any personal questions.

If this story illustrates anything it is: 'Don't wait to be asked'! Be yourself from day one, talk about your life away from work, your interests and your family. It will create bonds and make you a far richer, more interesting person to your colleagues.

When you merely play a part at work, and use only a fraction of yourself, you hold back from fully engaging with your work, your colleagues and with life. Bringing your home self to work means being your whole self all the time. And to do this, of course, you need to know yourself, and to connect your heart and your head. It involves integrating the warmer, kinder, more easy-going aspects of yourself with the sharp, alert and decisive aspects.

This kind of integration is far less exhausting than the personality switch that so many people go through every day, and far easier to achieve than you might imagine. When you hold back a part of yourself from those you work with, you are playing it safe and attempting not to stand out. But this is illusory, for the safest thing to be is yourself and the open and honest course of pinning your colours to the mast is always the most satisfying and successful one.

> When Ian Chisholm, chief executive of Columba 1400, was working for the American Management Association and leading their Operation Enterprise (Young People's Leadership Training Programmes) he was invited to give an address to a Congress of Native American peoples. He wondered how he should dress, and eventually decided to go along as a 'typical American of his generation'. But when he arrived he found the Native American delegates in full and formal dress. He began to regret his decision to dress down and just be yet another American.
>
> The following year he was invited back, and this time he made no mistake. Instead of dressing to fit in with the crowd he decided to reach back with delight into his Scottish ancestry and he wore Highland dress – a kilt. Not only did he feel more comfortable but the Native Americans clearly did too, and warmly welcomed him as a representative of his nation:

So often we think it more appropriate or safer to blend into the crowd and to avoid standing up as our true selves. Yet all the while there may be those, such as the Native Americans in this story, who wish us to be ourselves and so to remain different.

Exercise

Who are you at home and who are you at work? Write two brief descriptions of yourself as you imagine others see you. For the first, place yourself at home, and for the second be at work. How much do these descriptions match one another? Which qualities and personality traits do you present at home and which at work? Are there distinct differences?

It would be interesting to show these pen sketches to close colleagues and those at home for their reactions – though there is no obligation to do so. The real value of the exercise lies in what you discover about yourself and the differences you identify between your behaviour at home and how you are at work.

A WHOLE NEW YOU

When you integrate those parts of yourself that you leave at home each day with the parts you take to work, the benefits are many and marvellous. Some clients have described this transformation in terms of feeling that they are making a fresh start and becoming a whole new person. Your view of your job, the part it plays in your life and the role you play at work will all shift into a more positive light. You are likely to look forward to going to work far more than you used to, and to arrive without the tension and rigidity which may have characterised your 'dual-role' days. You will find it easier to inspire others and to bring out the best in them. You will also find it easier to bring out the best in yourself, rising to challenges, making decisions and moving forward with more energy than before.

This last point is particularly significant. It actually takes a great deal of physical energy to hold yourself rigid and tense for a large part of each day. And if you are behaving very differently at work from the way you behave at home, you are almost certainly very tense. Sectioning off parts of your personality in this way is exhausting and uses energy which could be put to far better use in helping you to do your job more effectively.

Of course we all present a front, to a greater or lesser extent. But relaxing that front, and letting others see the human being behind it, is the aim of integration. Taking your home self to work means letting your colleagues see more of what matters to you, what you really think about things that matter, and what your hopes and dreams are.

This poem, 'The Invitation', was inspired by the words of Oriah Mountain Dreamer, a Native American Elder, in May 1994. It perfectly sums up the aspects of ourselves which truly matter, the substance behind the veneer which we present as our lives and the wish we all have to know one another's deeper aspects.

It doesn't interest me what you do for a living.
I want to know what you ache for,
and if you dare to dream of meeting your heart's
    longing.
It doesn't interest me how old you are.
I want to know if you will risk looking like a fool for
    love,
for dreams for the adventure of being alive.
It doesn't interest me what planets are squaring your
    moon.
I want to know if you have touched the centre of your
    own sorrow,

*if you have been opened by life's betrayals or have
   become shrivelled and closed from fear of further
   pain!*
*I want to know if you can sit with pain, mine or
   your own,*
without moving to hide it or fade it or fix it.
*I want to know if you can be with joy, mine or your
   own;*
*if you can dance with wildness and let ecstasy fill you
   to the tips of your fingers and toes without caution-
   ing us to be careful, to be realistic, or to remember
   the limitations of being a human.*
*It doesn't interest me if the story you're telling me is
   true.*
*I want to know if you can disappoint another to be
   true to yourself; if you can bear the accusation of
   betrayal and not betray your own soul.*
*I want to know if you can be faithful and therefore
   trustworthy.*
*I want to know if you can see beauty even if it's not
   pretty every day,*
and if you can source your life from God's presence.
*I want to know if you can live with failure, yours and
   mine,*
*and still stand on the edge of a lake and shout to the
   silver moon, 'Yes!'*
*It doesn't interest me where you live or how much
   money you have.*
*I want to know if you can get up after the night of
   grief and despair,*
*weary, bruised to the bone, and do what needs to be
   done for the children.*
*It doesn't interest me who you are, how you came to
   be here.*

*I want to know if you will stand in the centre of the
    fire with me and not shrink back.*
*It doesn't interest me where or what or with whom you
    have studied.*
*I want to know what sustains you from the inside,
    when all else falls away.*
*I want to know if you can be alone with yourself;
    and if you truly like the company you keep in the
    empty moments.*

The poet wants to know who you are rather than what you
are, and what sustains and motivates you rather than what
you have achieved outwardly. These are questions it is wise
to ask oneself, too, in the quest for self-knowledge. Liking
yourself, knowing yourself and feeling at peace with who
you are is the basis of integrating your home and work
personalities and finding the courage to take your home self
to work. By following this path you will make deeper and
more meaningful connections with others and find it easier
to encourage and inspire them.

Susie was keen to leave school at sixteen, to the consternation of her
parents. She had not found anything which made her want to stay on and
study further, despite the fact that she was a brilliant and gifted all-rounder.

Then one day her German teacher asked her to have coffee with him
after class. This was unusual, but Susie liked the teacher and recognised
his love for his subject. The teacher was of German descent and had
suffered greatly as a naturalised British citizen, albeit a child, during the
Second World War. His accent and appearance were the butt of many
classroom jokes from his students. When Susie sat down he told her: 'If
we work we could go to Cambridge.' She realised he wasn't actually offering to accompany her, but offering help and encouragement – he believed
in her and wanted her to know it.

Susie did indeed go on to study German at Cambridge, after which

> she became a specialist in German literature and a public speaker of some
> note. Now in a very senior position, she pays tribute to what she calls 'the
> divine spark, or moment, when a great educator had the courage to break
> the mould and bring his energy and belief to someone in his charge'.

Most of us can look back at a special person who has
encouraged and inspired us at a key point in our lives. Which
of us wouldn't wish to pass on that encouragement to someone else as they reach a decisive stage in their own development? Yet it can never be done from a one-dimensional
stance. It will only ever succeed if it comes from an integrated
self, a whole heart, a whole personality and a whole self.

Exercise: the KWYA Test

This KWYA test (you can pronounce it 'choir', because it
asks what song you are singing in your life and work) is
great fun. It is a wonderful way of recognising your own
talent, ability and interests. I have used it many times with
clients and on leadership courses, and it never fails to produce
amazing results.

In this exercise, which works excellently around a dinner
table, those present are divided into pairs, each person team-
ing up with someone they don't know well. They are asked
to talk to one another for the duration of the meal and to
find out as much as they can about the other person. Each
person then introduces the person they have been convers-
ing with to the group, summing them up under the following headings:

K   Knowledge, skills and talents
W   Wealth of experience and shared wisdom
Y   Your values in life and in work
A   Aims and ambitions

Listening to someone else announcing to a group your skills, talents, experience, values and dreams is a powerful experience. Many people feel it sheds a totally different light on the way they see themselves, and the most common reaction is, 'Is that really me?'

> Greg was a company man. He had worked for the same organisation for many years with dedication and loyalty, and had risen through the ranks to a senior position. He had a wife and a daughter, but had always put work before his family life and was known for being last out of the office as well as for his rather dour style.
>
> When Greg announced one Friday that he was leaving at 3pm to see his fourteen-year-old daughter perform in a musical at her school, jaws dropped around the office. Some even wondered whether he was having a crisis of some kind. There was no crisis, but there had been a radical decision. Greg had been on an Away-Day at which we did the KWYA test. He heard his dinner partner describe his deep love for his daughter and it left him stunned and with a great deal to think about. He realised he had told a stranger something his daughter herself might not know – that she mattered to him more than anything else. He also realised that his dour style was in large part due to the resentment he felt at his daughter's life passing him by. Greg decided it was time to reorganise the priorities in his life, and his early departure that Friday was the beginning of a series of changes which left him a more open, warm and happy man.

BRINGING THE HALVES TOGETHER

So how do you go about bringing your softer, more rounded and warmer 'home' self into your working life? What is needed in order to make this change? Some clients have said to me, 'It's all very well in theory, but what do I actually do now? I've been the same person at work for twenty years – I can't just walk in as another person.'

This is true, and I am not suggesting an instant 'makeover', or leaving as one person on Friday and arriving as another on Monday. The process of integrating your home self with your work self is gradual and requires time, thought and effort.

It begins with thinking about what you like best about your home self and which characteristics you would most like to take with you into your working life. After that, it is a question of making gradual changes. For instance, remembering the doorman or receptionist's name and enquiring about his or her health, rather than rushing straight past, head down, towards the lift. Or perhaps making your next meeting less formal and more relaxed. Or cutting back on caffeine, which gives you headaches and creates tension, and keeping a bottle of water on your desk instead. Bringing your home self to work is about being a little softer around the edges, more open, more generous and more understanding. It means really looking at and listening to your colleagues at work and being willing to share some of yourself with them.

To do this you need to let go of the armour plating and be more human. Don't be afraid to ask for help, to admit that you don't know everything and to work with others as a team. Don't be afraid to laugh, to take and give advice and support, and to be generous with your time and your interest.

Ten Simple Ways to Take Your Home Self to Work

1. Put people first
Make connections with those you work alongside and encounter in your day by smiling, talking and asking questions about them. Notice if someone has a new hairstyle, a great tie, a piece of important personal news.

2. Practise relaxation
One of the things which can make us more rigid and limited

at work is physical tension. To reduce it, try some simple relaxation exercises and deep breathing.

3. Have great expectations

If you arrive at work expecting the day to go well, you are more likely to be cheerful and optimistic and to arrive smiling rather than frowning.

4. Allow for error

No matter how good the day, there are always things which will go wrong. Meetings run late, people make mistakes, deals don't come off. If you allow for this in your thinking you will be able to take it in your stride and keep your cool.

5. Do the unexpected

Change the pace and lighten the atmosphere at work by doing the unexpected from time to time. Give a small present to someone who deserves it, give everyone the afternoon off, take colleagues out for lunch, suggest an office outing . . . the possibilities are endless.

6. Give recognition

Appreciate and recognise the efforts of those around you. Don't take anyone for granted. Thank them for what they do and praise good work when you see it.

7. Personalise your work space

You spend a lot of time at work. Make your space, however large or small it is, your own with photos, cuttings, flowers or ornaments which appeal to you.

8. See the funny side

Whatever happens during your working day, there is always humour to be found if you are ready to look for it.

9. Share your news

If something has happened in your life, especially something good, tell others and let them enjoy it too. A child's exam success, a great day's golf, a race won – whatever it is, people will enjoy hearing about it.

10. Keep things in proportion

Work is not all there is in life – it is not even the most important thing in life, by a long way. So don't let work rule your life. Whatever happens in your day, remember that stressful anxiety rarely solves a problem and never balances a life.

> Alec was a manager who kept his home and work selves firmly divided. He was known as a good-hearted man by his family and friends, but at work he was a bit of an ogre. He had recently been promoted to department head and, feeling a little out of his depth, took this responsibility very seriously. He arrived early and began the day by chastising anyone who was even five minutes late. He worked hard and expected his staff to do the same, but he seldom gave any praise if they did. Instead he noticed every tiny error and had a knack of making people feel small and foolish. His critical, demanding style left his staff feeling nervous, diminished and wary. Most of them began to look for other jobs.
>
> When I met Alec he was puzzled about the fast turnover of staff and declining performance level since his arrival. It took a little while for him to see the effect he had unwittingly been having, but once he did he was keen to change. I suggested that the first thing he did was to stop looking for errors and start noticing what people did right – for instance, all those people who arrived on time, rather than the one or two stragglers. He agreed to give praise wherever it was due and to foster a more generous attitude to his staff. Within a couple of months Alec was reporting a marked improvement in morale and productivity in his department. He improved things still further when he began rewarding good work by giving his staff a monthly lunch and instituting more flexible working hours.

Benefits all Round

Not taking your home personality to work with you, then,

is not a good idea. Of course, there are those amongst us who could benefit from reversing the process and bringing our work selves home. Occasionally one comes across someone who is more relaxed, cheerful and pleasant at work than at home. But this is rare. For most of us it is the home personality which is more at ease, more open, more perceptive and more generous. These are all qualities which bring enormous benefit to the work environment. Taking your home self to work is well worth any effort involved and will bring rewards in terms of increased goodwill, productivity and performance.

chapter 5

Everyone Matters

When my three great-grandfathers set up their respective businesses around 150 years ago they must have faced many of the same challenges that anyone setting up a business or other enterprise faces today. One of the most important of these is finding others who will work with you and with whom you can create a relationship of trust, cooperation and loyalty.

All three were men of principle, for whom a handshake of agreement was worth more than a signature on a piece of paper and for whom honesty and loyalty were paramount. And all three understood that if the people who work for an organisation are looked after and feel part of it they will stay, their contribution will grow, and a sense of belonging and ownership will steadily develop. Their working ethic was that 'everyone matters', and it is as true today as it was then. Each of us needs to remember that all those working with and for us are entitled to respect, consideration, care and compassion, just as we are ourselves. In this chapter I will expand on the principle that everyone matters, and explain how we can practise this principle in our daily working lives.

Each of my great-grandfathers had a marvellous story to tell. John Walker began as a baker, but seized upon a new idea – that sugar cane could be refined in a factory in the port of Greenock on the river Clyde. John Walker & Co. Ltd became very successful, and many years later was bought by Britain's major sugar producer, Tate & Lyle.

John Denholm was nineteen when his father died and he and his elder brother James had to support their widowed mother and younger brothers and sisters. John decided to become a shipowner and placed a ship agent's plate on the door of a small office in Greenock. When he spotted a 72-foot-long sailing schooner, the *David Sinclair*, tied up in the quay and for sale, the young man approached a local banker to request a loan to buy it. But the banker told him, 'Run along now, and come back to me when you are a proper age to discuss such matters.'

Walking disconsolately along the main street in Greenock John came across two distinguished local businessmen, a Mr Black and a Mr Morrison, whom he told about the *David Sinclair*. The two men asked to go with him to inspect the vessel and, having done so, agreed to go into partnership with him. That was in the summer of 1866. Ten years later John Denholm was the proud owner of twelve schooners which plied between Greenock and Europe, Newfoundland, the West Indies and other parts of the world. The confidence which Mr Black and Mr Morrison had shown in him was rewarded by his success.

John Drummond, the third of my great-grandfathers, knew

poverty in his youth and set out on foot, pushing a cart containing all his belongings, from Glasgow to the burgeoning port of Greenock. There he realised that he could train as an apprentice cooper, making the barrels which were essential to contain the sugar, whisky and grain which were being transported to all corners of the British Empire and to bring back sugar cane and jute for sacking. Within a few years John had set up his own very successful cooperage.

DOES THE SHIP SMELL RIGHT?

All three of my great-grandfathers passed on plenty of sound common sense and wisdom about what makes a business successful. But the most outstanding of their principles was that the most important person in any business is the newest and youngest apprentice. What they meant was that responsibility comes before privilege, and that no matter how fortunate we are we should never forget our 'common humanity'. My great-grandfathers believed that in any business, no matter how new or how young an employee, that person mattered just as much as everyone else and should be treated with the same respect.

This principle has remained with me all my life, and has been my most valuable aid in the many and varied jobs I have been asked to do. It was reinforced when, at the ridiculously young age of thirty-two, I was invited to become headmaster of one of Scotland's most distinguished schools, Loretto in Musselburgh, near Edinburgh, the oldest independent boarding school in the country.

It is sometimes whimsically said that behind every good man is an astonished mother-in-law, and this was true in my case. The astonishment extended to my father-in-law, who, being of a certain type and vintage, never once complimented me, or any of his own children, on any achievement. For him, and so many like him, praise was the absence of criticism. He did, however, give me some unforgettable words of advice when I took over my new job: 'Norman, you must remember that when an admiral goes on board a ship he can tell almost immediately whether it smells right. Businesses, corporations, universities and schools are just the same as ships – when all is not well they don't smell right. And just like fish, when they go off they rot from the head down.'

This advice was enormously useful and since then I have asked myself on many occasions, 'Does the ship smell right?' And I have found that the only effective way to answer that question is to spend time in different parts of the organisation, including canteens, mail rooms and reception areas. If things are wrong in such key areas they are likely to be wrong elsewhere. If the staff in these areas feel overworked, unappreciated or ignored, the whole will not function effectively. And if this is the case the problem lies not with these workers but with the head of the organisation, who is not running things effectively or paying attention to what really matters.

In his famous poem 'If', Rudyard Kipling said, 'If you can walk with kings and keep the common touch . . . you'll be a man my son', and he was right. No matter how rich, successful or high-powered you may become, if you don't care for those who work with, under and around you you will not be able to create a well-balanced, harmonious and productive organisation.

Perhaps one of the most outstanding examples of a leader who kept his standards and thus prevented his expedition from going off and rotting from the head down was Sir Ernest Shackleton, the Antarctic explorer. *Shackleton's Boat Journey* by F. A. Worsley, his skipper on the epic journey towards the South Pole, and the more recent *Shackleton's Leadership* by Margot Morrell and Stephanie Capparell, bear out this principle again and again.

There is a touching and inspiring passage in *Shackleton's Boat Journey*: 'There was nothing to suggest to the outside world that Sir Ernest Shackleton and his men were near the South Shetland group; rather would they look for us in the southern part of the Weddell Sea. There was no hope of rescue by others.

'Plainly, the thing to do was to take a boat to the nearest inhabited point, risking the lives of a few for the preservation of the party.

'It was certain that a man of such heroic mind and self-sacrificing nature as Shackleton would undertake this most dangerous and difficult task himself. He was, in fact, unable by nature to do otherwise. Being a born leader, he had to lead in the position of most danger, difficulty and responsibility. I have seen him turn pale, yet force himself into the post of greatest peril. That was his type of courage; he would do the job that he was most afraid of.'

WHEN THE ROT SETS IN

Organisations and businesses which value every member of staff tend to be successful and to have satisfied, loyal workers who stay with them and who believe in the goals of the company. On the other hand, organisations where those at the top don't care about those below tend to have a fast turnover of staff and to breed discontent and lack of effort. If staff are struggling, feel unnoticed, have no support or are out of their depth they will become unhappy and leave.

Some organisations believe in a fast turnover of staff and that it is not worth investing time or effort in their workers. One such company was a large publishing house. The managing director was arrogant and dismissive, and had no time for the problems of staff below senior management level. Staff at more junior levels felt they were left to sink or swim, that no one cared whether they stayed or went, and that they were simply there to give their pound of flesh. A small handful were picked out for promotion, but the rest were ignored.

For several years this policy seemed to work reasonably well. The publishing house brought in good profits. But bit by bit things went wrong. A rival publisher came into the market from overseas and became known for its loyal, caring and supportive attitude towards staff. Gradually, as the best staff moved from the first publishing house to its rival, profits in the first company dropped and the second flourished. It was only when the long-standing and uncaring managing director moved on that the first publishing house began to change its ways and to clear out the rot which had set in from the top down.

The shipbuilding yards of the Lower Clyde are a powerful example of what happens when the principle of 'everyone matters' is not applied. In the early 1970s I was asked by the management of Scott Lithgow shipbuilders and the Presbytery of Greenock and Port Glasgow to conduct a survey into why the shipyards had two thousand vacancies which they couldn't fill. This was at the time when the oil industry in north-east Scotland was getting going, and of course many skilled workers were lured away by higher wages and better housing. But that alone did not explain the huge number of vacancies in an area where there was plenty of unemployment.

Any visitors to the shipyards at that time could not have failed to notice how often the self-destruct button was pushed. Despite the best efforts of management, during the worldwide depression in the 1930s, to keep the yards afloat and literally to feed families, a great deal of enmity and distrust from previous conflicts remained. This attitude was undermining the entire industry, as certain key workers and influencers were still mutually hostile and uncooperative. At a time when unity was vital, there seemed to be those who were still intent upon division. It was sad to see this happening in yards that had once built the finest ships in the world, while at the same time the Japanese and Scandinavian shipbuilding industries were leaping ahead.

As in many other industries, tales were handed on from generation to generation in Clydeside. Many of the tales were of misery and humiliation. One told of how in earlier days the foreman, in a bowler hat, would blow a whistle for a ten-minute tea break. Then, just as the water in their billy cans was coming to the boil on the men's braziers, the bowler-hatted figure would blow the whistle and kick the cans over into the fire with the cry, 'Back to work, you lot.'

The memory of this kind of cruel and inhuman behaviour, albeit from times gone by, set up a powder keg of bitterness, anger and hurt, which ultimately played a large part in the decline of the shipyards. Things could have been very different if working practices had been more far-sighted and concerned with the individual wellbeing of the workers, and if the valuable part that every single person has to play in any organisation for the common good had been more widely recognised.

The study of corporate histories reveals many organisations where those further down the ladder have not been properly treated or recognised for their talents and abilities. The closer you got to the top, the more you mattered, and the signs of this were everywhere. In one particular bank the directors had individual towels hung on individually initialled towel hooks in the gentlemen's lavatory close by the board room. In another major institution, plain china was for those at the bottom of the board room table, china with a silver rim was given to those in the middle of the table, and then, for the 'holiest of the holy', there were a very limited number of plates with a gold rim! Such exclusive practices naturally led those who were excluded to ask if they really mattered in the organisation or would ever be good enough to count.

No wonder then that Max De Pree, in his outstanding book *The Art of Leadership*, compares and contrasts such attitudes with more forward-looking companies such as the USA furniture giant, Herman Miller, where there is a common canteen available to all, visibly exemplifying the available share ownership of the company. Also interesting in this regard is how one of the world's largest pharmaceutical companies, Novartis, refer to everyone throughout that large and expanding organisation as Novartis Associates.

THE WAY FORWARD

The principle behind the statement that 'everyone matters' is that everyone has something of value to offer, talent to be developed and a contribution to make. If you are able to make people feel good about themselves and what they can offer, you will make them successful both for you and for themselves. Treating everyone in your organisation with equal respect, courtesy and belief in their potential is the way forward for any business which wants true success. And this begins with sharing the organisation's achievements and giving everyone a sense of belonging and ownership. No matter where you are in the hierarchy it is vital to treat those you work with in a decent and generous manner, giving thanks, encouragement and support where it is due.

Here are my five simple rules for keeping the 'everyone matters' principle flourishing.

1. Encourage

Never underestimate the power of encouragement. The right words spoken at the right time will be remembered long after you have spoken them, and may change the course of another person's life. We all remember someone who has been a mentor to us, showing belief in us when perhaps no one else did, leading us in the right direction and giving encouragement when we weren't sure whether we could achieve the next step. Are you prepared to go the extra mile that considerate leadership requires?

It is important to remember, too, that encouraging is not the same as lecturing. Some words of St Augustine are very pertinent here. He said, 'I learned most not from those who taught me but from those who talked with me.' If you want to encourage, a genuine exchange of words is often far more effective than a one-sided talk or explanation.

> One of my own mentors was George Thomas, Viscount Tonypandy, Speaker of the House of Commons between 1976 and 1983. George rose from a Welsh mining background to become Speaker at the invitation of two governments of different political hues, led by James Callaghan and Margaret Thatcher respectively.
>
> Everywhere George went he was renowned for his 'common touch' – the ability to realise that in any organisation everyone matters and that a word of kindness and encouragement can so often provide inspiration just when it is needed. He came often to Loretto when I was headmaster, and the school's foremost awards are now called the 'Lord Tonypandy Awards for Leadership and All-round Contribution to the Life and Wellbeing of the School'. On one occasion George spoke at a packed school service, after which he was mobbed by students, staff, parents, grandparents and godparents. He had time and a word for everyone. Someone remarked afterwards that 'When he spoke to you, it was almost as if you were the only other person in the room or in his life at that particular moment.'
>
> One evening George and I arrived at the chapel to find that it was being adapted to accommodate the set for a major school musical production of the opera *Dido and Aeneas*. Working late into the evening was a senior student, a boy who was by no means a strong academic, nor a talented athlete, singer or actor. But he was one of our best all-round contributors, always available to help and attentive to a fellow student or member of staff in need.

> George spoke to the boy for a little while, at the end of which he stood back and said, 'Well then, young man, I can tell you one thing. You are going to lead a very useful life.' And so he has. To this day he remembers George's words of encouragement, which made him realise how much he mattered and how important his contribution was, both in school and beyond it.

The Tonypandy test

And so let us apply the Tonypandy test. If you were given a relatively short briefing about an individual in your office, shop or factory, would you be able to show interest and encouragement in the life of that person? Would you leave them feeling good about themselves and their contribution? Would you enable them to fulfil their potential and achieve their best? Asking yourself what it would involve, on your part, to do this, and whether you have the energy, goodwill and sensitivity to encourage others, is the starting point for recognising that everyone matters.

The right words

Appreciation is another powerful form of encouragement. Noticing and praising what someone has done, and rewarding their efforts, is a wonderful way of strengthening working relationships and creating loyalty.

> John Marshall, chief executive of the furniture company Durham Pine, is a great example of a man for whom everyone matters. He took everyone who had worked for the company for more than a year, 162 in all, plus their partners and children, on a week-long holiday to Majorca, paying the costs of flights and accommodation himself. On top of this, the break was not deducted from the staff's annual leave. His extraordinary gesture was a thank you after the company posted a record profit. Mr Marshall, who joined his employees and their families on the holiday, said, 'When I first started working I felt unloved and unrespected. Now that I am on the other side of things I don't want my employees to feel the same.' One of his staff, a senior sales consultant, said, 'It's nice to get some

> sort of thank you for all the work we've put into the company, but this is really above and beyond anything we could have hoped for. There are a lot of smiling people around here.'

Imagine the bond and the sense of loyalty and commitment that the staff at Durham Pine must have felt after this kind of recognition by their boss. His heartfelt gesture will have positive repercussions which will last for years. His entire staff will almost certainly have felt encouraged, both personally and professionally.

Make sure those who work with you feel appreciated for their efforts. A word or gesture can make an enormous difference when someone has put in effort and deserves recognition.

2. Expect the Best

What kinds of expectations do you have of those who work with you? Do you look for faults, or do you expect the best?

This is an interesting question to ask yourself, because finding fault can become a habit that we barely notice. A great starting point is the way you behave towards yourself. Do you mentally list the things you missed, got wrong or could have done better each day? How often do you notice how many things you did well in a day and give yourself a pat on the back?

If you are harsh with yourself, you may well be the same way with others. If so, try to break this particular habit, because routine fault-finding is damaging and morale-destroying. It will leave others feeling that when they are around you they can never get anything right. Soon they will feel there is no point in even trying, because only their mistakes will be noticed. And eventually they will want to move departments, transfer to another branch or leave the company altogether. Expecting the best means looking for success. Be ready to spot someone doing something right or well, rather than the opposite, and then comment on it as soon as you see it. The people around you will be quick to notice, and will respond by doing even better.

> Katie's story is a great example of the difference that expecting the best can make to a young person. It was as a homeless, unemployed girl of eighteen that she arrived at our Columba 1400 centre on Skye with a curtain of hair over her face – we could hardly see what she looked like. It was as though Katie didn't want to face the world, and this was hardly surprising since she had had an extremely harsh upbringing in which she had never known praise or encouragement. For three days Katie continued to hide behind her hair, as she and the other young people who had arrived with her went through their leadership academy course. This is a course that aims to bring out the best in each young person: the facilitators are on the look-out for talent, ability and skill, and are quick to praise.
>
> Then, after three days, Katie asked to borrow a hairband and pulled her hair off her face. It was as if the curtains had been drawn back as she realised that she was trusted and respected. She saw herself clearly for the first time, as did those around her, and revealed herself to have a real talent for conflict resolution.
>
> By the end of her course Katie had discovered that what mattered to her was cruelty to animals. On her return she started to work as a volunteer at an animal refuge centre. So good was she that it was not long before she was offered a full-time paid job, and now Katie is not only in employment but has also found herself a house and is in a steady relationship.

3. Never Diminish

How constructive are you when you need to check or criticise? Are you quick to find fault, to criticise in public or to send hasty emails pointing out errors and misjudgements? When you work with 'everyone matters' as a guiding principle it is important to consider carefully before making negative comments or criticisms. Words spoken or written in haste can have a long-lasting and damaging impact on others.

Use the following guidelines for critical feedback:

- Give such feedback only when you feel it is necessary and appropriate.
- Never act in haste. Think for a while before responding.
- Keep your criticism specific. Address only the person or people directly involved, and discuss only the deed or event which is relevant. Generalisations such as 'You always . . .' or 'Every time . . .' are usually inaccurate and only increase the damaging effect of your words.
- Be clear about the behaviour or action you expect in the future. Explaining what someone has done wrong is not especially helpful, whereas telling them what you would like them to do to get things right gives them clear guidelines.
- Never use personal criticisms or put-downs. Stick to criticising an action or behaviour rather than the person. For instance, 'I don't like it when you arrive late' rather than 'You're no good at time-keeping.'

A young Scottish schoolboy scored 57 not out in his Saturday morning cricket match. Immediately he phoned his American grandfather – it was still night over there, and he was woken by the call. Yet the grandfather still switched on to the high excitement of his grandson, who exclaimed, 'Grandpa, I played cricket this morning and scored 57 runs not out.' To which the grandfather said, 'That's fantastic! Keep at it and you'll soon be playing for Scotland.' And of course the young boy went out and practised again and again and scored many more runs and soon began to dream actively of playing for Scotland.

But as far as his Scottish grandfather was concerned, he had to wait until the regular Sunday evening telephone conversation, as this grandfather did not welcome impromptu calls. On being told of the boy's cricketing achievement he replied, 'And how many chances did you give?' No recognition or praise was forthcoming, and when the boy put down the phone he felt sapped and dispirited.

So often we fail to realise, when we are in any position of

authority, how deflating our words can be. The boy's Scottish grandfather did not intend to demean or discourage his young grandson. But by his attitude, looking for fault rather than offering encouragement, this was the end result.

Discouragement is a bit of a British disease. It is sometimes referred to as Tall Poppy syndrome – if you stand above the rest you will get cut down more quickly. We are quick to say, 'Don't get big-headed', 'Who do you think you are?', 'Don't get above your station' or 'What makes you think you're special?' But such remarks put people, and in particular the young, 'back into their boxes', discouraging their potential and destabilising their eagerness to do well. Perhaps it is time we began turning these unkind phrases around and encouraging those who do well to feel pleased, happy and inspired.

Write to praise, speak to criticise
An exercise worth building into your daily, weekly or monthly plan is that of 'write to praise – comment or check in person'.

It is all too common these days for comment and criticism to be sent in the form of an email. Not only can this type of missive often be read by others, but its impersonal tone is demoralising. The recipient can read it over and over again, convincing themselves of their lack of worth or success and further demoralising themselves. Those who write to criticise or condemn rarely find that they achieve anything like the intended outcome. On the contrary, this approach can often lead to the poisoning of relationships. That email or letter stands there as a visible and tangible testament to perceived inadequacy, fault or breakdown in communication.

In contrast, a quick and to-the-point personal comment is effective and more easily dealt with. The working relationship will not be impaired and the recipient will not lose dignity or a sense of worth. Taking the trouble to speak frankly and empathetically with those who need help or a clearer sense of direction is rarely wasted.

Writing is, however, entirely appropriate when you wish to praise or appreciate someone. The value of a note, email or letter saying something positive is enormous, and the fact that it can be saved and reread will only boost the recipient's self-esteem and commitment.

> When I was a headmaster I was stopped in the corridor one day by a very distinguished, long-serving schoolmaster who was about to retire. I had just written to thank him for his years of valuable service in the school and to tell him how much he would be missed. He told me, 'I have never been very good at expressing my feelings, but I can't thank you enough for taking the time and trouble to write to me. You see, I have a drawer where I keep such letters. It's not a very big drawer, but it is to that drawer that I return from time to time to realise that perhaps, after all, my life has been worthwhile and I have made a difference.'

Some of our greatest leaders throughout history, from President Abraham Lincoln to Dr Arnold, the legendary Headmaster of Rugby School, to Field Marshal Lord Montgomery of Alamein, have been those who have taken the time and trouble to write to individuals to thank them and to praise them for significant contribution and effort. Even if you are feeling too busy or too stretched, remember that a single hand-written line will still make a significant difference.

4. Delegate

One of the best ways in which to let someone know that they matter is to give them responsibility. Many people have discovered the very best in themselves while meeting the challenge of new responsibilities and tasks. Yet plenty of people in senior positions are surprisingly reluctant to delegate. Never make the mistake of being the kind of person who has to do everything themselves and who tries to stay in total control. Be willing to spot potential and to encourage it by setting tasks which will stretch and challenge people.

I have often coached chief executives who are worn out and stressed because they have so much to do. Yet when we examine their workload we discover that there are plenty of tasks they are hanging on to which could be passed down the line and which others would enjoy doing.

Good communication is a vital part of delegation. When irritable executives tell me that someone down the line has messed up on a job, the first thing I ask is whether they have clearly explained what they expect and what is involved. All too often they have left the other person guessing part of the story.

> When I am coaching a client I often suggest, three to six months into the process, that we meet their line manager and hold a three-way conversation. Recently I had a meeting with a client who worked for an airline and her line manager, who happened to be the chief executive officer of the company. My client had told me what she felt was expected of her in her role as head of acquisitions. However, during our open and frank three-way conversation the CEO outlined a very different version of the role he expected my client to play. Unable to hide her surprise, my client said, 'I never knew you saw it that way,' to which the CEO, also surprised, replied, 'But I thought I'd told you how I felt.' These two people had had numerous meetings and yet had not achieved clear communication about the role my client was expected to play. After that three-way meeting relations between the two were warmer, my client felt able to carry out her role with far more confidence, and the CEO increased his trust in her.

If you want a job done well, always be absolutely clear about what is involved and what you expect, and update this information regularly. In this way delegation becomes something which benefits both sides and leaves people feeling they are trusted and able.

5. Stay In Touch

Leaders and managers who retreat into ivory towers, never seeing or speaking with those further down their organisation, make the mistake of losing touch with the 'feeling on the ground'. How can you know how people feel, what matters to them, what the energy of the organisation is like, if you don't stay in touch? The best leaders and managers always live by the principle that they would never ask anyone to do something they would not do themselves. And they are willing to demonstrate this on a regular basis.

> When I was a young chaplain with the Black Watch we were sent to the Brecon Beacons for training. On the first night there was heavy snow and a fierce blizzard. Even the Royal Marines came off the mountains that evening, but such was the regimental pride of the Black Watch that we pressed forward and even the mess waiters, who could have been forgiven for wanting to turn back, marched into the teeth of the gale.
>
> On that long, cold night I set out to try to visit each company location and found the commander of Bravo Company, Major Edward De Broe Ferguson, huddling on his own in the Company Command post. For camouflage reasons he needed to be there, active and available on the radio. Only when I joined him did I realise that the water was well above his ankles.
>
> As I made my way around the various slit trenches of Bravo Company I found that none of the men were actually in their trenches. When I asked why I was told, 'Because the major said so, padre. Unless on stand-to, the major's orders are that no one is to remain in their trenches if the water is above ankle height.' I mentioned to the soldiers that I had just visited the major, who was up to his knees in water, to which they replied, 'That's Major De Broe, padre. You see, he would never ask us to do anything that he wouldn't be prepared to do himself.'

I found that within the army's regimental system everyone did matter, and the men who became outstanding leaders knew this and lived by it every day. Perhaps one of the most brilliant Black Watch officers was the late Brigadier Tony Lithgow, a man of superb tactical skills whose men so respected him that they were quite prepared to die for him. History relates that Tony would always conclude his briefings to the men by saying, 'The question we must ask ourselves is: "Are we ready for war?"'

On one particular occasion when the Black Watch had come off exercise, all the armoured personnel vehicles and all members of the battalion were on parade in the vehicle park ready for the Commanding Officer's inspection. Many hours had been spent on bringing the vehicles up to his high standards of inspection and cleanliness. That is, all bar one which had been left in a prominent position; inscribed in the caked mud on its sides were the words, 'We're almost ready, Tony!'

EXERCISE: THE COURTESY TEST

How much genuine consideration for others do you show? Do those who work with you see you as someone who values them and treats them with respect and goodwill? Give yourself this little courtesy test as a measure of your good manners and consideration for others. Once a week, or more often if you are able, think of someone who works with you and for whom you are responsible within the organisation. Ask yourself the following questions:

- Have I been courteous, considerate and kind towards this person?
- Do I know how many cylinders they are firing on right now, and why?
- Do I enable them to bring their home personality to work?
- Do I encourage them to use their abilities and reach their potential?
- Have I made a positive difference in their life?

If you can answer yes to these questions, you pass the courtesy test with flying colours. If not, use these questions as standards and aim to increase the number of 'yes' answers you can give within the next week.

> One particularly wet evening I was making my way down the steps of Waverley Station in Edinburgh in order to catch a train to Glasgow. The rain was so heavy that it was bouncing off the pavements and soaking those unlucky enough to get caught in it. In front of me and going at a speedy pace with a splendid umbrella – I had, alas, failed to bring one – was a typical city gent in a well-cut pinstripe suit. At that moment I saw him veer across the steps to where a homeless young man was sitting cross-legged and becoming wetter by the second. In a trice the umbrella switched hands from the suit to the down-and-out – whose need was greater by far.

This story is a wonderful example of true courtesy in action, devoid of fuss or any need of acknowledgement.

AT WORK AND AT HOME

'Everyone matters' is not merely a principle of good business practice. It can also be applied, with great effect, to your domestic and personal life. Our three eldest children, Andrew, Maggie and Marie Clare, were born over a period of four years. Some six years later Christian was born. With the first batch of three children, when we were very much a team of five, it was easy to feel that everyone mattered. Yet when Christian came along, such was the pace of family life and the noisy demands of three very extrovert and different older personalities, that this small boy found it very hard to have his stories listened to or his jokes laughed at. His deep inner agony was further compounded when Elizabeth and I were daft enough to produce another, instantly attractive and increasingly active, son, Ruaraidh, some seven years later!

It has taken Christian considerable time to realise his strong and natural place within the family unit, and it has also cost his mother and father dear to learn where, despite our best efforts, we have been found wanting in our parenting skills. Of course Christian always mattered just as much as the other children, but what we didn't at first realise was that he didn't feel he mattered. It is not enough to know that someone matters to you – you need to make sure that they know it and that your behaviour towards them demonstrates it. I am glad to say that Christian is now a very dynamic young man whose principled stand for truth and justice hugely impresses not only his parents but also his brothers and sisters.

Ultimately the company or organisation or family that fails to recognise that each individual matters, and to understand each individual's abilities, needs and place in the whole, may find themselves dealing with a range of problems. It will be well worth the effort in the long run to address such situations swiftly and honestly. It is a wise person who recognises, as Mr Black and Mr Morrison did with my nineteen-year-old great-grandfather, John Denholm of Greenock, that everyone, no matter what their age or level of experience, has something valuable to contribute.

chapter 6

Don't Collapse the Tent

*t*There are few times more challenging than when you are taking over in a new job, after a promotion or move. This is the time when nerves are jangling, your stomach is churning and doubts and fears set in. 'Am I up to it?' you think. 'What if they've made a mistake in appointing me? What if I blow the whole thing? I feel out of my depth.' These doubts and fears are natural and a certain amount of nervous adrenalin is a good thing because it will motivate and drive you. But if panic sets in you will be in danger of messing up, quite unnecessarily, and making your worst fears come true. This is when it is time to make sure you don't 'collapse the tent', and in this chapter I will show you how to cope with the nerves and worries which set in when you are faced with a new job or a new challenge. I shall give you a guide to coping calmly, successfully and confidently with whatever is ahead.

'Don't collapse the tent' is a favourite saying of mine, one I use a lot when coaching or running leadership seminars. For most of the people I work with it resonates immediately and, while it causes some amusement, it is also extremely useful. In fact recently the human resources director of a leading UK utility company told me that 'Don't collapse the tent' had been the single most helpful principle in the drive towards improved practice in her organisation.

So what does 'Don't collapse the tent' mean? Well, think of what happens when a tent, especially a very large one such as a marquee, is put up. The canvas is spread out over a large area on the ground and then, working together, a number of people pull on the ropes and the tent goes up, providing light, space and cover for those within. Now think of the recently promoted senior manager or executive sitting on top of the tent. He or she is supported by the canvas and can happily stay aloft, climbing carefully down one of the guy ropes from time to time to see that all is well. But if he or she panics and starts to struggle – afraid that they will fall off, uncertain about whether the structure will hold them up and nervous about how to get down – the tent will collapse.

So what happens when the tent collapses? Everyone is in chaos, not knowing what they should be doing, uncertain about what has happened and what is needed next, and fed up because the tent was doing fine before the oaf on top collapsed it. It is almost as if the air of creativity and energy has been sucked out.

Now think of the tent as a working organisation. The behaviour of the man or woman sitting on top of any particular part of it is vital to the smooth operation and continued stability of the whole. If he or she starts to panic out of inexperience or doubt, then everyone in the organisation will feel the impact and the damage can be considerable.

Those who collapse tents often don't realise what they are doing until the damage is done. And it is all too common for someone who has been newly promoted to a senior position to feel insecure and so collapse the tent.

Here is a wonderful example of what happens when a tent is collapsing and confusion reigns.

Everybody, somebody, anybody and nobody
There was an important job to be done and everybody was sure that somebody would do it. Anybody could have done it but nobody did it. Somebody got angry about that because it was everybody's job. Everybody thought anybody could do it but nobody realised that everybody wouldn't do it. It ended up that everybody blamed somebody when nobody did what anybody could have done.

OVER-CHECKING

How do you collapse the tent? By getting tied up in the detail of the job, nit-picking, over-controlling and trying to do everything yourself. Constant checking and balancing kill inspiration and enthusiasm. When you are in danger of collapsing the tent you are likely to be fussing over people's shoulders, refusing to trust them and insisting that they fill in reams of paperwork or report back to you at every move. It is exhausting and demoralising, for you and for them.

Are you a tent-collapser? Do you drive those around you mad by checking and more checking, and so demotivate and de-energise those who look to you for a lead? Answer yes or no to the following questions to find out:

1. Do you know exactly who in your organisation to trust to get a certain job done?

2. Do you dread the number of tasks you have to perform and the long hours needed?

3. Do you feel confident that those around you can do their jobs well?

4. Do you feel you must check every stage of the process?

5. Are you able to focus on the end result and leave the details to others?

6. Do you feel you need to be an expert in every area?

7. Do you believe that you can confidently handle the demands of your job?

8. Do you sometimes wonder whether you are right for this job or should perhaps have stayed in your old job?

9. Do you feel that you can handle a crisis, should it arise?

10. Do you wish, at times, that you had someone to turn to for advice, but feel there is no one?

If you answered no to two or more of questions 1, 3, 5, 7 and 9, or yes to two or more of questions 2, 4, 6, 8 and 10, you are on your way to being a tent-collapser. Don't panic, however, because the majority of those who are promoted into managerial jobs feel the same way and experience these same doubts, worries and fears.

A most likeable and talented client of mine who worked within the careers service told me that her goal was to be promoted and to test out her skills and experience in a larger arena. Soon after this she received her promotion, which was to a very senior position with direct bearing and influence on the formation and conduct of government policy. She had deservedly achieved the early aims of our coaching programme. Once the celebrations were over, though, she began to feel uncertainty, if not panic. She told me that she felt she was not respected for her knowledge in the way that she had been in her former role. Everywhere she went others seemed to know more than she did. 'It's worrying me so much that I seriously wonder whether I was right to apply for this job and to accept it,' she said. 'Perhaps I should consider asking for my previous one back? My husband and children were so happy and proud of me, but now this new job is eating into our family life. What shall I do?'

This was a woman who felt out of her depth and who was clearly in danger of collapsing the tent. It took her a little time to calm down, take a deep breath and adjust to her new role, but with a little support and guidance she was able to do so and to begin enjoying herself.

So what should you do when you feel you are in danger of collapsing the tent? How do you adjust and earn the respect and loyalty of the people you work with? The strategy you need is surprisingly simple and straightforward. Remember, first, that in order to operate at your best in the work environment you need to know and trust yourself, allow your head and your heart to connect, and go forward with this self-knowledge and inner connection as your firm foundation.

HOLD FIRE

The first step when you feel uncertainty or panic setting in is to hold your fire and do nothing. Don't rush about trying to find solutions or quick fixes – simply go for a little time out, take a few deep breaths and ground yourself.

When we panic we move into our heads and lose our connection with the ground beneath our feet. Oxygen fails to reach the brain and spiritual energy fails to reach the soul. This connection keeps us calm and solid, so it is important to take a little time to renew it. Breathing deeply helps you to do this.

Rushing around trying to be everything to everyone is simply a waste of your energy. It advertises the fact that you are on edge and feel you can't cope. Staying cool, calm, grounded and quiet will immediately give you an air of competence and authority and will convince you, and others, that you are fine. To give the impression of being cool and calm, even if this isn't how you feel, use the following guidelines:

the Spirit of Success

- Remind yourself that you know who you are and have your head and heart connected. Act from this strong base.
- Slow your pace a little and breathe more deeply, so that you walk, move and speak with measured care rather than hastily. When you enter a room for a meeting, pause before you begin to speak.
- Speak less rather than more. Listen to what others have to say and think carefully before you respond.
- Dress smartly and with care, to make a good impression.
- Be polite, interested and courteous to everyone.

If you are faced with problems, the 'hold fire' principle can be very useful here too. If others around you are panicking, complaining, agitating and urging you to solve all their troubles, resist the urge to dive in and just stand back from it all.

Sick All Over You

This is the term I use when people can't wait to unload and dump on you. It is graphic, but it is also apt, because being on the receiving end of someone else's complaint can indeed feel as though someone has been sick all over you.

Leaders, executive and managers often have to deal with this kind of thing. Someone arrives for a meeting in an agitated state and can't wait to tell you how angry they are. They bubble with indignation, upset, a sense of unhappiness or inadequacy – and they go on and on. So what do you do?

You may be thinking, 'Help, what can I do here? I can't sort this out.' But what you do, outwardly, is stay calm, listen and say as little as possible. Within a short time the aggrieved person will finish, and if you don't engage with them and begin an exchange they will have nowhere to go with it. At this point they are likely to stop and either calm down or leave. At times like this, holding fire is powerful, authoritative and effective.

Harry was a partner in a legal firm and was still very young when he was promoted to managing partner. The other partners were all older than him, some much older, and Harry felt very anxious about whether they would accept him. He began to rush around trying to justify his promotion by doing too much. In this way he lost his focus and his ability to make good decisions. He acted too fast and was in danger of alienating the older partners, who watched him with some amusement as he began to flounder.

When Harry came for coaching he was deeply anxious and wondered if his promotion had been a mistake. However, in a very short time he began to turn things around by stepping back and holding fire. He learned to be more measured and to choose carefully when to get involved and when to leave things alone. He also stopped actively seeking the approval and respect of the other partners and learned to trust his judgement and to respect himself. Things steadily improved, Harry's confidence grew, and he knew he had made it when one of the most respected and senior partners told him, 'I wasn't sure about you at first, but you've proved me wrong.'

DON'T TRY TO BE AN EXPERT IN EVERYTHING

When people move up a rung at work they often feel that they ought to know, in expert detail, about every tiny nut and bolt of their new job. But this is both impossible and unnecessary. No one can be or should be an expert in all the fields involved when they have wide-ranging responsibilities.

If you are in this position you are there to give an overview and to bring the whole together, including the expertise of others in their individual areas of responsibility. Your job is to view all your responsibilities one by one, and assess them calmly, strategically and well. Then you can gradually become more conversant with each part of your organisation or enterprise. You can defer to those who know more than you do about specialist areas without loss of face. It is a wise person who is able to admit their own shortcomings and ask for help, advice or direction. Make sure that others see you as an enabler and appreciate the encouragement you give them, rather than dreading your visits or meetings. You have absolutely no need to know the day-to-day responsibilities of all those who work with you. What matters is that you trust them and make their jobs as easy, pleasant and effective as possible, by allowing enough light and air into the tent.

In one of the world's greatest engineering companies there remained until recently a heavy and outdated culture in which line managers reported in intricate detail to the general manager at monthly meetings. The atmosphere of these meetings was intimidating, and the line managers felt like nervous children waiting outside the head teacher's study for punishment. They dreaded these meetings so much that their husbands and wives came to dread them too, and even their children knew that 'something was up' at that time each month. The scenario created was very much 'them and us'.

Without realising it, and from the best possible motives and intentions, this particular general manager was in fact 'collapsing the tent'. He was knocking all the stuffing out of the well-intentioned men and women who were reporting to him. It took some time in the coaching situation for this general manager to realise how suffocating his approach had been and to decide how he could begin again without losing face.

Looking at himself and at his past enabled him to realise that his greatest need was for recognition and commendation on his accuracy of detail. His older and supposedly brighter sister had been so favoured by their parents that the only way he could make his voice heard was by getting things absolutely right as often as possible. This accuracy of detail had been noted by a later mentor in his life, who saw it as a talent and encouraged such an approach. Work, as in his earlier family life, therefore became something of a contest. But this approach was clearly not working for the line managers who had to face being pulled apart at the monthly meetings.

The general manager's approach made it impossible for those he worked with to see his 'home' personality. They could not see his dry wit and sense of humour. They had no idea that he had a passionate interest in football coaching for young people. They didn't realise what a kind and loving father he was.

It took time and courage for the general manager to change his approach, but over a period of months he did so.

He had taken the time and trouble to get to know his senior players better. Now, instead of the dreaded monthly meeting, he holds a briefer and far more relaxed meeting and follows it up by dropping in on each of his managers to see where he can offer them support. 'How is it all going?' has replaced 'Why hasn't this been done by now?' 'How can I help you in your work?' has replaced 'That's ridiculous – it was never that complicated in my experience.' He has learned to give and accept support, and to trust his managers to know their jobs and do them well.

DEVELOP HELICOPTER VISION

When Sir Bob Reid was chairman of Shell UK he gave an impassioned and impressive lecture to a gathering of head teachers and career counsellors at the University of Aberdeen. He recommended a concept which he called 'helicopter vision'. By that he meant that anyone who takes responsibility for others should from time to time imagine they are getting into a helicopter and flying above their place of work. In this way they can look down and see the whole, with all its parts operating together.

Helicopter vision lifts you above the petty, the mundane and the ordinary, enabling you to expand your vision and clarify your goals. You can see far more clearly who is doing what, where things are getting stuck, what needs to be done next, and what adjustments you need to make in order to keep the whole operation flowing smoothly.

When I became BBC National Governor and Chairman of the Broadcasting Council for Scotland at a comparatively early age, I felt the loss of day-to-day control and hands-on responsibility. What did it mean to be a chairman as opposed to a chief executive? I was soon to learn, for whilst the Controller of BBC Scotland was dealing with many decisions each day and keeping in touch with all his departments on a weekly and monthly basis, my job was very different. It took me a little while to understand that my main task was to encourage the increasingly impressive BBC Scotland and give it as much space, air and light as possible. In that way so much of what was already well placed in expert and experienced hands could flourish in even more productive and creative ways.

BE AN ENABLER

If your job involves responsibility for others, you are in a position to be an enabler. To enable others means to encourage and nudge them in the right direction so that they use their own skills and abilities to the maximum.

When you do someone else's job for them you dis-able them. How can someone show you what they are capable of if you don't give them the chance? If you are leaning over their shoulder, picking up on every tiny mistake, waiting for them to mess up or telling them how to do it, you dis-able. But if you give them clear guidelines about what you want done, encourage them to believe they are capable, trusted and up to the job, and then let them get on with it, you are enabling. Let people know they can come to you for advice if they need it, and then take your focus off what they are doing.

When you delegate, you not only enable others but free

yourself. An unwillingness to delegate indicates insecurity on your part. Be willing to let others shine, to take pleasure in their success and to let them face challenges in their work. If you enable others, therefore, you reap benefits yourself. By enabling you build a stronger team, inspire confidence in others and free yourself to concentrate on what you really need to deal with.

> Ted was a broker, bright and full of promise, but he had no concept of working in a team. Although full of ideas about strategy, marketing and administration, he thought them up only for himself.
>
> When Ted was promoted, the problem got worse. A number of people were responsible to him, but he had no idea how to handle them or bring out the best in them. Instead he continued to behave like a one-man band, doing everything himself and leaving his team feeling unimportant and ineffectual. This meant that Ted became more and more unpopular, and several of the people working for him applied for other jobs. He also became increasingly tired and stressed. It was only when his own boss sat him down and pointed out what he was doing that Ted began to make changes.
>
> With the careful guidance of a boss who was herself a great enabler, Ted learned to appreciate, value and inspire others. He began by seeing each member of his team and getting to know their strengths and areas of expertise. His next step was to delegate more, handing over responsibilities to the team members and learning to trust them. As the team members' confidence and enthusiasm grew, so did Ted's. By handing over work he didn't need to do himself he gave his team members a boost and himself more time and space for the things he needed to do.

SAVE YOUR ENERGY

Nothing is more tiring than running around trying to do everyone's job for them and to be everywhere at the same time. Rather than doing this, conserve your energy for the appropriate moment. There will come a time when it is crucial that you step in and deal with a major issue, and being ready for such an eventuality is far more important than trying to deal with every minor issue which presents itself.

Not only does tent-collapsing make you less effective at work, it also impacts deeply on your home life. When the ace education service client I mentioned earlier commented upon how tired he had become, how his work/life balance had been shot through and how his wife and children were increasingly unhappy, what was he saying? Simply that all the energy required for the major decisions, not to mention for being a husband and father, was being used up in collapsing the tent. He was overburdening himself and depleting his energy levels by spending far too much time trying to get up to speed with a large number of intricate issues and areas.

By deploying helicopter vision and not collapsing the tent, his morale and energy have been restored. In fact he has become confident and dynamic and is now running one of the most focused, ambitious and technically sharp departments within his highly influential organisation.

EXERCISE: BE A MOUNTAINEER

Living and working surrounded by the stunningly beautiful mountains on the Isle of Skye, I have become well aware of the bond that exists between mountaineers. On occasions these men and women have to make life-or-death decisions and to rely absolutely on one another as well as on their own judgement. The recognition of these crucial decision-making areas for those who aspire to reach the summit of a mountain gave rise to the following two exercises.

Sharing Your Rope

A phrase which mountaineers frequently use is: would you share your rope with him/her?

By this they mean, would you trust this person with your life? When you choose to climb a mountain with a partner, or team, you share the rope, and in so doing you share responsibility for one another and for the final outcome. Sharing a rope with someone means trusting that person absolutely.

This exercise involves identifying key players within your organisation whom you can rely on and with whom you can share vision and values. With a small handful of such people in place you can form a rope-sharing team that is strong and sound enough to climb the challenging mountains of the tasks and goals ahead.

Ask yourself:

- Who would I share a rope with?
- Am I failing to notice people who are more than capable of sharing the rope with me?

This is the first step towards building a team you like, trust and enjoy working with.

Placing Your Pitons

Pitons are the pegs which climbers hammer into crevices in the rock face to use as steps. The piton is a vital part of any rock climb and is deployed carefully, thoughtfully and tactically at the most important times and places on the ascent. Only a limited number of pitons can be carried in a rucksack and they can only be used one at a time, so the choices each climber makes about when to use them are critical. The 'piton moment' represents the opportunity or occasion when you must dig in, take a stand or make an important decision for the continuity, welfare, policy and advancement of your organisation.

Just as the mountaineer can't hammer in all his pitons at once without ruining his climb, so the wise manager will realise that timing is everything and you can only use one piton moment – that is, make one decision, stand or choice – at a time. By clearly defining your route in this manner, all those sharing the rope with you, and some further down the climb, will see clearly what you mean, what you stand for and where you are leading.

To be truly effective you must use your piton moments sparingly and with maximum impact. Don't waste them on minor decisions or situations which others can manage or resolve.

Ask yourself:

- When did I last use a piton moment to maximum effect?
- In what situations might a piton moment make a real and lasting difference?

A recently appointed university principal who came to me as a client had realised that the legacy of a previous administration needed a lot of sorting out. More effective decision-making and clearer leadership were called for. Constant management by consensus had merely led to an atmosphere of increasing uncertainty and instability in many departments and areas of university life. The new principal's temptation was to roll up his sleeves and become actively and intricately involved. But he understood that by doing this he would collapse the tent, so he chose a different approach which was soon welcomed by the university staff.

The first question the new principal asked was: 'Who would I share a rope with?' He soon discovered that there were a number of key players who, with his confidence in them, could begin to form a strong team. By identifying them individually, listening to them and to their hopes and aspirations, and then sharing his vision and values with them, the principal was able to put together a strong team.

As the reorganisation of the team and the refocusing of the management of the university began to take place, he began to focus on the use of his 'piton moments'. The principal was careful to be sparing and to consider maximum impact when making decisions or announcements or formulating new policies.

KEEPING THE TENT UP

To keep a tent standing strong and stable, it is necessary to ensure that every peg that keeps a rope taut is properly in place in firm ground. Running a department or a business is no different. It is the job of the person in charge to make sure that everything is running smoothly and in place. If you panic, others will soon sense it and panic too. If you keep calm and confident they will pick up on this and feel more confident themselves. It is all too easy to begin collapsing the tent when you are unsure. The trick is to use all your inner resources to deal with your own uncertainty, rather than allowing it to grow or passing it on. Knowing yourself, keeping your heart and head connected, trusting your own ability and judgement and taking things at a calm pace will ensure that the tent remains up and ready to face whatever storms and tempests may arise.

chapter 7

Self-appraisal:
How Am
I Doing?

*i*In the workplace, most of us either appraise others, or are appraised by others. This process is an integral part of working life and can be extremely valuable. We wait to be told how we are doing and then tend to accept what we are told, even though the appraiser might not know us well and might miss vital areas of our potential and ability.

Self-appraisal is doubly valuable. It is all about having the courage to look long and hard in the mirror and note what you find there. Yet how often do we turn the spotlight inwards and assess ourselves? How often do we honestly and openly ask ourselves what is working and not working in our lives, what we are good at and which areas of our ability need strengthening, how far we have come and where we want to go? For most of us the answer is seldom or never. Yet when self-appraisal becomes a habitual part of your life it can be enormously helpful in creating the kind of life you want to live and the work you want to do. It becomes a tool you would not want to be without.

In this chapter I will be looking at what is involved in self-appraisal and encouraging you to develop the self-appraisal habit so that it becomes an automatic part of your life. If getting to know yourself is the first step, then self-appraisal is the second. By this means you can regularly update your self-knowledge and understanding of yourself.

Self-appraisal involves being clear, frank and truthful with yourself and then choosing the way you want to move forward and the goals which matter most to you. Self-appraisal means asking: 'How am I doing in my own eyes?' This matters far more than how you are doing in anyone else's eyes, because the first and last person you live with each day is yourself. If you feel good about how you are doing, if you like yourself, like what you do and believe that you do it well, you will develop a sense of confidence and ease with yourself which will draw others to you.

Using simple exercises and checks, I will show you how to appraise yourself and to use this process to move your working life forward in the direction you most want to go. I will also explain the importance of developing a personal code of values and of appraising yourself in the light of these values, and not the values of others.

If you appraise others, it is impossible to do so accurately if you are not willing first to appraise yourself. Without self-appraisal you will become inwardly lazy, willing to allow old, unhelpful behaviours and habits to predominate and to hold you back. Self-appraisal is a vital part of knowing yourself and connecting your heart to your head.

THE SELF-APPRAISAL CHECKLIST

Take a look at these ten questions and answer them as truthfully as possible.

- Do you like your job and want to go on doing it?
- Do you like the way you do your job?
- Do you feel good about the way you treat colleagues and those you are responsible for at work?
- Do you know what your short- and long-term goals are?
- Do you consistently adjust and review your goals?
- Do you feel that you continue to learn through your work?
- Do you look forward to the future?
- Does your working life balance well with your home life?
- Do you feel fulfilled by your work?
- Are you able to sort out problems as soon as they arise?

If you are able to answer yes to all these questions then your working life is in good shape. If there are any questions to which your answer is no, these areas need attention and deeper consideration. If you answered no to more than three questions, it is time to undertake a thorough review of your working life and to consider new directions and moves.

HOW ALERT ARE YOU?

Whilst serving as chaplain with the Black Watch regiment I remember on one occasion, on tour in Belize in Central America, watching the sergeant major of Bravo Company, Starchie Smith, taking an 'encouraging' drill parade in the cool early hours of a new day. 'You're not concentrating!' he shouted to his men. '*Be a-lert*!' After a short while, as the drill still didn't reach his standards, a frustrated Starchie bawled, 'You're still not concentrating! Be *a-lert*!' before adding, 'Come to think of it, you're all a bunch of lerts!'

This story has reminded me on countless occasions during individual coaching and in group sessions or conferences of the need to be *a-lert*, and from this has developed what I call the ALERT test. It is a model that has been particularly helpful to many Cap Gemini Ernst & Young (CGEY) Boardroom Excellence programmes on their ambitions and committed progression from Director/Vice President towards Partner/President of that world-famous and influential consultancy. I am also glad to say that it is a model which has been increasingly used by executives and staff at all levels in many companies as a guide to good practice and a readily available personal self-appraisal checklist.

As you go through the ALERT headings, ask yourself in what way they apply to you and your life. Let this take the form of a wide-ranging and detailed self-review.

A   Awareness of Setting

How much do you notice about what is going on around you at work? Do you notice when the person you are working with, negotiating with or giving instructions to is tired? Do you know when he has fallen out with his secretary, had a rough day or got problems at home? Are you able to take these things into account and make the necessary adjustments? Can you take five minutes out to offer support or simply listen? Awareness of setting is about seeing the broader picture and recognising what may lie behind what you see on the surface. How easy do you find it to do this? Are you sometimes like a steam train, rolling ahead despite altering circumstances which may require a different and more sensitive approach? To develop this kind of awareness start to notice the detail of what is going on around you. Look at the room, the people and the interactions, and then adjust your own behaviour and expectations accordingly.

A high-flying young Manchester consultant had been used to early success. The new project provided an even greater challenge. For him and his team it was something of a test of mettle, and one which could lead to further success and promotion. But he was anxious about the key meeting which lay ahead. When I asked him to describe this fear he explained that he found the board room, where the meeting was to take place, daunting, and was intimidated by the chief executive. He was worried that he would not do well in surroundings where he felt ill-at-ease and under the eye of a man he feared.

So far he hadn't done anything other than panic about this. But with a little encouragement he began to develop his awareness of setting. Only then did he begin to see things from the chief executive's point of view and to realise that, for him too, a lot rested on this meeting. He began to see the CEO as human and vulnerable. He then sketched the layout of the board room, so that he felt more familiar with it, and began writing down the odd key phrase which he could keep to hand to help him through the meeting.

As the time of the meeting approached he found that he felt ready and surprisingly calm. The result of this careful and sensitive preparation was a very successful meeting.

L   Left-Field

Are you confident enough to be different? To shift away from the run-of-the-mill response, to come up with a new way of doing things, to see what's going on from a fresh angle? The US baseball term 'left-field' aptly describes such thinking. Being left-field means resisting the predictable and looking for the approach which will make a difference, excite, delight and succeed. Looking at the left-field approach also means asking yourself how up-to-date you are with what is going on in the world. Are you in touch with all angles of news in the press, radio and television? Are you an interesting person to meet? The conversation you have over lunch or in a coffee break can make all the difference to the success of a meeting or project.

When sixteen-year-old Euan Blair, son of the UK Prime Minister, found himself tired, emotional and stranded in London's Leicester Square late one night, many a cry went up in British households. Who was supposed to be supervising him? What was he doing out and about at that time and in such a state?

You might easily term such comments 'expected right-field thinking'. They were repeated, and many more in the same vein, in press reports, social conversation and the round of business dealings and discussions. Yet the left-field comment waiting to be made was far more interesting. Young Euan Blair had been deserted by his mates and left alone in the centre of London. Where were they in his hour of need? Such a left-field comment can often inspire a far wider-ranging and more interesting conversation.

E   Energy

Do you understand your own energy patterns and how they affect you at work? Do you get energy 'white-outs' when you forget for a moment what you are doing? Can you read your own body clock, and those of others around you? What do you do about it? It is often easier and more convenient to indulge in some addictive habit (nail-biting, eating, drinking and so on) than to get to know and work with your own energy levels and body clock. Many unhealthy lifestyle habits are developed just to enable people to keep themselves going, working through pain and exhaustion to the point where they no longer recognise their own needs.

Are you fully aware of how your body clock ticks and when and where you are at your most effective? Do you take this thinking with you into conversations and meetings and deal-making conferences? As with the battery in a car, you cannot keep on recharging it ad infinitum. At some stage it will need renewing. A regular health check should be regarded as essential, and the resultant recommendations wisely and carefully acted on. By being just that bit kinder to yourself you can not only be at your best but also bring out the best in others.

A very dynamic magazine editor in his late thirties found to his surprise that he was beginning to feel consistently exhausted and under the weather. He had always prided himself on needing very little sleep, having fantastic energy levels and being able to work a twelve-hour day and then socialise for half the night. I asked him to begin reviewing his health and energy levels by keeping a journal for a week, detailing his activities and in particular energy low points, diet and exercise.

The result was fascinating. He found that he started the day full of energy but felt tired during the late morning and early afternoon and then picked up again by late afternoon. He got no exercise and was eating a poor diet – no breakfast, a lot of coffee, an over-large lunch and a very late evening meal, often accompanied by generous amounts of alcohol.

He didn't want to alter his lifestyle completely, but was willing to make adjustments in order to feel better. He began eating breakfast, cutting back a little on lunch and on the coffees, and having alcohol-free midweek evenings. He also began going to the gym three days a week after work, which he found he very much enjoyed. With these changes his health and energy levels improved. He also began to work with his energy lows, which still tended to be after lunch. He avoided scheduling meetings for these times, and did some less demanding work for an hour or so.

R Reviewing

Life is often about making deals. Are yours the kind you want to make and can feel good about? Do you take the time to review what is happening, even when you are in the middle of an important meeting? Do you look at whether everyone comes out of a negotiation with something to show and a sense of completion? Do you regularly review your progress with projects, relationships and goals?

One of the most helpful things you can do is to take a few minutes at the end of each day to review what has happened and decide what you are happy with and what you might want to change or do differently. This is not the same as endless anxious analysis. Review should take place from a position of quiet confidence and should not take more than a few minutes, after which you can set the issues aside until it is time to deal with them. Reviewing is closely allied to energy, because in order to review what stage you are at in a conversation or a meeting or even in the whole of your life, you will need to be aware of your energy levels, your body clock and the state of your health.

A young high-flyer in financial services was doing brilliantly in her career until she made a couple of major mistakes. First in one deal and then, soon afterwards, in a second, she brought in poor results. Worried that she was losing her good judgement, she came for coaching. When she arrived she was seriously wondering whether she should resign. She knew another mistake would lead to her sacking, despite previously excellent work, and was not sure what to do next.

As she went through the ALERT steps and got to the reviewing stage she began to understand what had gone wrong. She realised that on both occasions when she had made a poor deal it had been at the end of the day, when everyone was keen to finish, and she had pushed the result through because she was anxious. If she had been able to stand back and review the situation she might have chosen to bring that day's meeting to a close and arrange a further meeting to close the deal. This way she would have had a chance to rethink her approach and do a better deal.

From this point on she began to review meetings as they progressed, often taking a ten-minute break and going off for a quiet think before coming back to the table. Her next few deals came through with excellent results and she felt all her confidence return.

T   Timing

Do you allow yourself enough time to achieve what you want? Or do you rush, pack too much into too short a time, and end the day feeling exhausted and dissatisfied? Are you one of those people who is unrealistic about time, constantly trying to fit an hour's worth of activity into twenty minutes? Good timing is vital to the successful closure of any business deal or personal negotiation. It is also vital to creating a life which feels comfortably full and enjoyable rather than overburdened and exhausting.

When you learn the art of timing you will realise that you always lose when you race the clock with a never-ending list of things to fit in. The art of timing is to be realistic, to choose priorities and to know when to stop. So take a long hard look at how you use your time and what you might need to address in order to feel that the pace of life is right for you.

A young executive complained that he always felt in a rush, always under pressure to commit or to perform to an often unrealistic deadline. Though only thirty-three, he felt that he was living his life on a treadmill which was turned up too high – he was always running to keep up, and it was wearing him out. He liked his job but had lost all sense of satisfaction and enjoyment because of the breakneck pace.

Encouraged to take the ALERT test, he began to look at his attitude towards time. He realised that many of his deadlines were self-imposed and that the sense of burden he felt was increased by the fact that he took on more than he could comfortably cope with. He made a decision to look for ways to reduce his workload, and to allocate an appropriate amount of time to the tasks he needed to do. The result was that he felt more effective, less rushed and happier with his work.

He concluded that of all the stages of the ALERT self-appraisal test, perhaps timing has been of most help to him in his increasingly successful business career. By being and staying ALERT, by regularly doing the

> ALERT test in professional, business and personal situations, he has found himself growing as a person. More than that, he has actually enjoyed doing it and has rediscovered his sense of humour and spirit of fun.

For the ALERT approach to work you will require honesty, humility and, as Sergeant Major Starchie Smith liked to say to his men, you will need to be *a-lert*. Countless men and women have applied this test in individual encounters, during more formal meetings or at major events and conferences. Many have found a new level of personal understanding and awareness of others, and have been able to turn difficult situations around and to create better business and working relationships.

The ALERT test provides a readily available framework, easy to conjure up in your own mind and then to follow through. Developing the ALERT qualities will shift you towards working in a way which is more productive, interesting and satisfying. You will also learn to give others more freedom, to value their contributions and to encourage them to feel trusted. This in turn will enhance their performance, awareness and self-esteem and give them a far greater sense of enjoyment and purpose in everyday life.

BE TRUE TO YOURSELF

Self-appraisal needs to be carried out in the light of the beliefs and values which matter most to you. For instance, if you believe that everyone deserves to be treated with respect and courtesy, you will review your own behaviour towards others in this light. And if you find that you have fallen short of this standard, perhaps by harsh or thoughtless words or actions towards someone you work with, you will want to consider what is needed in order to adjust your behaviour. For example, you might have been overtired, stressed and under pressure, and this is what led you to snap at someone. The real adjustment needed here would be a look at how the pressures on you can be eased and you can get more rest.

It is important, then, to be aware of the beliefs and values which have meaning for you and which you would wish to live and work by. This becomes even more necessary when you realise that there will always be people who are critical and who wish to undermine you in some way. When you come across someone like this – and we all do from time to time – you need to hold fast to your own beliefs and refuse to absorb or act on anything which attempts to undermine you.

> As a headmaster I regularly had to say goodbye to those students who were leaving Loretto and going out into the world. I used to thank them for all that they had achieved and contributed during their time at the school, and would add a few words of advice which often left them looking startled and amused. What I told them was: 'When you set out to make a difference, don't let the beggars get you down' (they often used to change the 'e' and the 'a' to a 'u' and an 'e' for heightened effect, when quoting me on this advice!).
>
> What I meant, I explained to them, was this: 'There will always be those who think they have a better idea, who have been doing it first, or who are jealous of your initiative and enterprise if you set out to shape, create or contribute to something "out there". Never allow the tired, worn out comments of other people's indifference, sadness, jealousy or competitiveness to get you down or stop you from achieving what you set out to do.'

During one particularly difficult time at Loretto I remember my friend and mentor, Hector Laing, saying to me, 'Norman, why let the pinpricks of small minds get you down?' Anyone who has achieved anything of note will have had to bypass a few small minds on the way. It is up to you whether you let them stop you, or whether you smile politely and carry on undaunted, knowing that you are being true to yourself and that this is what counts most.

> In my time at the BBC, the membership of the Governors' Remuneration Committee went from four to eight. So important and at times contentious were the issues that eventually all the Governors served on the Remuneration Committee. I well remember that I sometimes needed courage to own up to uneasiness over the size of certain bonus awards. Often I would feel duty-bound, bearing in mind that the BBC is a public service corporation, to speak up when a huge increase was under discussion and say: 'Where I come from that sum of money could help to pay ten nurses or social workers or ministers or priests for an entire year.'
>
> It was never easy saying these things, though on several occasions the response seemed to be a tilt in the direction that I was suggesting. Nevertheless disappointment was ultimately always the result, as the Committee went ahead and awarded the bonuses. Sometimes there seemed to be a tacit acceptance that what I was saying was right and true, but that market considerations in terms of competitive salaries obscured those views. None the less I did at least feel that I had done my best to bring my colleagues' attention to another point of view and to stick to the values which I believed in.

Sticking to your values and beliefs won't always make you popular, or make life easy. What it will do is give you a strong sense of who you are and where you are going, and ultimately it will lead to greater victories.

> The story of Eric Liddell, the 'flying Scotsman', is a wonderful example of sticking to one's principles in order to achieve even more. In the 1924 Olympic Games in Paris he refused to run in the elite 100 metres event, which was to be held on a Sunday, because it would mean he would not be keeping the Sabbath. When the devout Liddell was encouraged to run instead in the 400 metres final, a note was passed to him by one of the greatest American athletes of the day quoting the biblical text 'Those who

honour me, I will also honour'. Liddell, who had enormous mental and physical discipline and was also an international rugby player for Scotland, went on to win that 400 metres Olympic Gold Medal. The event has since been recorded in the Oscar-winning film *Chariots of Fire*.

THE COLUMBAN CHALLENGE

At Columba 1400, our international Leadership Centre in Staffin on the Isle of Skye, a very simple code of values has been embraced for those who come to us to learn leadership skills. We call this the Columban Challenge. It is about self-appraisal, asking yourself how you are doing and how you can further raise and realise your hidden potential. The motto of Columba 1400 stems from the writings of John Buchan on the Marquess of Montrose. In 1644 Montrose, a famous Scottish general who supported the Royalists in the English Civil War, gathered together what was termed a 'rag, tag and bobtail army' and defeated the much larger opposition forces, known as the Covenanters. Montrose's men succeeded against the odds largely because of his clear leadership and lifelong belief in the rich potential of each and every human being. 'Our task,' he said, 'is not to put the greatness back into humanity but to elicit it, for the greatness is there already.'

The Columban Challenge, therefore, is based on the belief that we all carry greatness within us. Over the last few years representatives of many organisations, from Ernst & Young consultants to Halifax Bank of Scotland trainees, from Rolls-Royce apprentices to Lloyds TSB bankers, have taken the Columban Challenge into their working and personal lives as a self-appraisal tool that can be used at any time.

Under six headings, the Challenge asks you to consider your values, beliefs and goals as you review your working life.

the Spirit of Success

Awareness

Self-awareness is the starting point and the key to recognising your own beliefs and values. When you are willing to turn the spotlight inwards, you demonstrate courage. It is not easy to face your own shadow side, but self-awareness necessitates looking at all aspects of yourself. Through it you will discover what is truly important to you.

Focus

Once you know what is truly important to you, you can begin to focus more clearly on it. What do you wish to move away from, and what do you wish to achieve? Once you focus on what matters to you, your energy, ideas and motivation will follow.

Creativity

When you are fully aware and focused, the need for thoughtful action becomes apparent. Through this action we reach deep inside for the inner creativity which enables each and every one of us to be special and to make a difference.

Integrity

Without integrity, no code of values will stand up to the scrutiny of challenge, conflict or changing circumstances. A deeply rigorous and shining integrity is essential as you travel the road of self-awareness and of contribution to others.

Perseverance

No great task or undertaking in life, no great achievement, no great foundation or discovery was ever achieved without a core of perseverance. If you are truly to realise your potential and the greatness in you, you must remember that failure is very often the bedrock of the next success. Only through perseverance can the strength and integrity of our character shine through.

Service

The aware, focused, creative person of integrity and perseverance will find themselves indubitably led to the service of others. One of the marks of greatness is the willingness to serve. Nelson Mandela, the first black President of South Africa and a man of extraordinary courage and integrity, said in a tribute to his great friend and mentor Walter Sisulu, 'By ancestry I was born to rule. Walter helped me to understand that my real vocation was to be a servant of the people.'

The Embodiment of the Columban Qualities

Having used the Columban Code to ascertain or reconfirm your values, you may well find yourself wishing to be a stronger, kinder and greater presence and personality in the lives of others. Certainly for the young people who come to Columba 1400 it can act as a beacon, showing them a future they had never thought possible.

> Tommy was a young man who came to Columba 1400 from Glasgow. He had been abused from an early age in a children's home and had gone on to become a heroin addict. After almost a decade on heroin he was now a stabilised methadone user. Before he came to the centre Tommy was only able to leave his house for twenty minutes each day to collect his methadone prescription. He was filled with self-loathing and felt there was no hope and no future for himself. By the end of his stay with us, his fear of speaking to people had gone and he had discovered that he wanted to make a contribution and to help others. Tommy now works in a charity shop in Glasgow and spends his free time knocking on the doors of his neighbours seeking clothes and toys for the children of Afghanistan.
>
> On his departure from Columba 1400, Tommy left a handwritten note

> which said: 'Thank you. I have preferred heroin to my daughter Siobhan for the past twelve years. I am now going back to her and to her mother to try to rebuild our family.' And he has.

A man who clearly embodies the Columban qualities is Sir Edmund Hillary, who, with Sherpa Tenzing, conquered Mount Everest in 1953. At an official reception to mark the fiftieth anniversary of the men's climb Helen Clark, the Prime Minister of New Zealand, referred to Sir Edmund as 'the best known New Zealander in the world' and said of him, 'What he represents to us is vision, courage, perseverance and integrity. I believe that goes a long way to explaining why he has inspired our people for half a century.'

HOW YOU ARE, NOT WHAT YOU SAY

At a time of crisis the chief executive or chairman or headmaster or principal or director general or senior consultant very often has to face the music of a gathering of staff, shareholders or media, either internally, externally or both. At these times, if you are an experienced leader you will realise that poise, bearing and style carry enormous weight.

In general, people may be looking less for expert guidance than for a sense of uplifting confidence and trust in your leadership. For instance, if you have appeared on television, a friend or family member who has watched you is more likely to report on your appearance and bearing than on your words. If you were to ask them whether they remembered what you were talking about, they would almost certainly say, 'I can't remember exactly what you said but you were looking good (or tired or whatever).' In leadership positions, it sometimes does you good to remember that, however careful you must be with what you actually say in public and its potential consequences, you are frequently being judged on how you are. For this reason it is useful to look closely at your style and bearing. Use the following guide to enhance your sense of authority and self-confidence in demanding situations:

1. Make sure you dress suitably and look well groomed.
2. Move slowly. Rushing into the room conveys a sense of panic. Walk calmly and at a measured pace.
3. Pause. Use the art of pausing before you speak to enhance the power of what you say.
4. Look around at everyone present and smile. If you do so, you appear self-possessed and confident.
5. When you speak, keep it relatively brief and to the point.

DO WHAT YOU HAVE ALWAYS WANTED TO DO

Very often we discover, when doing exercises such as the ALERT or the Columban Challenge, that there are blocks which we are putting in our own paths, sometimes unwittingly, sometimes knowingly. What is getting in the way of you having what your heart deeply desires? Almost certainly the impediment is of your own making, even if it does not appear to be so.

Ben Zander, the highly talented and intuitive principal conductor of the Boston Philharmonic Orchestra, uses his musical skill to illustrate the kind of blocks we commonly self-impose. He plays a particular piece of music on the piano, first as an eight-year-old might, then as a thirteen-year-old might, then as an adult might, and finally as a concert pianist might. At every stage there comes a point at which Ben says to the audience, 'And now I am reaching the difficult bit.' It is his contention that, whatever the age or stage we are at, and even if we possess the skill of a concert pianist, there comes a moment when we tell ourselves, 'And now I am reaching the difficult bit.'

The first task in the recognition and discovery of blocks which we ourselves put down is to accept them and to realise that we are not alone in this thinking. Do we, however, wish our lives to be predicated on our own feelings of self-inadequacy or the doubts, fears and criticisms imposed upon us from childhood by others? Finding the courage to identify the blocks will allow you to begin to remove them and open the way to reaching your dreams and goals. Look at the key issues in your life and decide what new habits are required to bring about more satisfying results. What beliefs and practices might you begin to change for the better?

WHEN THE GOING GETS TOUGH

There is no greater test of mettle than when things get really difficult. When you carry out a self-appraisal, ask yourself how you react when the chips are down and the going gets tough. Do you panic, blame someone else and run? Or do you face the difficulties head on, grit your teeth and come through stronger and wiser?

In the Parachute Regiment, where the sense of belonging and commitment is a powerful incentive, they use a wonderful saying: 'You're never as tired as you think you are.' The motto of Gordonstoun School is very similar: 'Plus est en vous' (There is more in you). Both are useful thoughts to keep to hand in those moments when you feel you are up against enormous odds, or running out of resources and energy.

When I left the Parachute Regiment, which was at that time a mere forty years old, I joined the Black Watch, senior Royal Highland Regiment, then 240 years old, and it was not long before I felt embraced by their special brand of loyalty and tradition. The relationship between officers, non-commissioned officers and private soldiers was like that in a very close-knit family and invariably shot through with wit and good humour.

There are few better places than the armed forces to learn just how much you do have in you, way beyond the moment when you feel you simply can't go on. And there is no greater sense of fulfilment and satisfaction than the one achieved at the end of a feat of physical or mental endurance. For every leader, or would-be leader, there are times when the strength of your resolve is tested, when you must face potential defeat and still carry on towards victory. These are the times which define us, and which, when we have come through them, carry us on to greater things.

THE SELF-APPRAISAL HABIT

Unless you begin to ask yourself 'How am I doing?' or 'How can I make a better contribution?', tired and worn out habitual behaviour is likely to predominate. We all get into routine and unthinking habits unless we choose to examine our own behaviour and choices. Your personal code of values will lead you to a self-appraisal test of your choosing which can be regular, reliable and reassuring. Self-appraisal will keep you on track and become a valuable tool as you continue to discover who you are and what you might yet become. Self-appraisal is personally valuable, and a great example to others. At its best, it is a wonderful opportunity to ask yourself those questions which others might never ask.

chapter 8

Power
and
Responsibility

*P*ower and responsibility are inextricably linked at every level, both in the context of work and outside it. We all have some level of power. Even the newest trainee has the power to do a job well or badly, to respond to requests with good will and effort or to withhold and disrupt, to grow and develop their potential or to waste it.

As we move up the career ladder responsibility increases and so, accordingly, does power. We begin to take responsibility for the work and development of others and at the same time to have a certain amount of power over them. Later we are given positions which carry increasing levels of power. And with great power comes great responsibility. Spiderman's Uncle Ben got it right, and every good executive knows it.

To have power is to have a position of influence or

authority. To be responsible is to have the ability to respond appropriately to any given situation and to be morally accountable for your actions. Ultimately responsibility is the wise, thoughtful and caring use of power. Unfortunately, those who gain eagerly sought after positions are often far too aware of the privileges that come with such promotion and ignore the responsibilities. When this happens, the result can be damaging both to the individual and to the organisation.

In this chapter I will discuss the use and misuse of power and the responsibility we all have to ourselves and to others. I will also ask the ultimate power question: Are you a leader? Take the Leadership Moment Test and find out whether you have graduated to true leadership status, with all the power and responsibility that this entails.

Not all of us are destined to be leaders. Recognising when you have reached the level which is right for you is a key moment for anyone, and a self-empowering decision to make. Not every manager makes a good executive; the wise ones know the difference, in others and, most significantly, in themselves.

THE MISUSE OF POWER

To misuse power is to fail to meet one's responsibilities towards others, and this kind of failure is sadly all too common. Many of those who hold power in the workplace misuse it by threatening and abusing their staff. This is sometimes done subtly through the use of a look or tone of voice, at other times by shouting and haranguing.

Barbara was the editor of a national woman's magazine. Dynamic, charismatic and glamorous, she exuded confidence and would enter the building each day like a whirlwind, barking orders, calling meetings and issuing changes and alterations to the previous day's decisions about the layout and appearance of the magazine: Barbara had moved from one magazine to another, lured by grateful publishers who knew her reputation for increasing the circulation and profile of any magazine she headed.

There was, however, another side to Barbara, one which the publishers never saw but which her quaking staff knew only too well. She was moody and changeable, and could be charming and cruel by turns. No one, not even her most trusted staff members, knew which side of her they would get on any given day, or even from hour to hour. She was heard yelling the most appalling abuse at her department heads and, although everyone joked about it behind her back, they also dreaded encounters with her. One day she told an assistant editor who was late for work, 'Do you know that no one round here likes you?' A couple of hours later she invited the same woman into her office for a friendly lunch. In the end most of the staff couldn't wait to look for other jobs. Barbara's undoubted brilliance was overshadowed by her vicious tongue and unpredictability.

Such behaviour is bullying, and undermines and demoralises those on the receiving end. Employees can't shout back at a boss, even if they want to. Those in positions of authority have a responsibility to behave with respect towards the people who work for and with them.

Consistency and predictability are also valuable qualities in someone who has power. When people know where they stand with you and what to expect, they are able to relax and get on with the job in hand. If they are constantly waiting for the next outburst or mood-change, they will be tense and on edge.

There is also another way in which power can be abused: if those in positions of power and authority place self-interest before the interests of others for whom they are responsible. Examples of this kind of misuse abound, as more and more of those at the top place the desire for self-promotion and personal wealth before all else. These people are willing to damage the jobs, families and livelihoods of others in the cause of their own pursuit of money and status. In many cases the dishonourable behaviour of such people is covered up by corporate boards intent on damage limitation and image preservation. Devices such as the blurring of accounts, the setting up of imaginary businesses and the hasty departure of 'fat cat' directors are used to cover the tracks of those who have abused their positions of power. These people then depart the company 'blameless' in the eyes of the law but damaged in everyone else's eyes and, one imagines, in their own consciences.

Of course, there are also those who make the mistake of putting self-interest first but who recognise it and are able to restore their integrity through subsequent actions. Such people can, in fact, be stronger and wiser for such experiences, with a greater sense of self-awareness and a greater understanding of the responsibility which comes with power.

Integrity is a little like a reed or a young tree. In high winds some break, but others bend with the wind and remain strong and able to stand again after the storm. Many great characters from literature and figures from history failed to rise to an early challenge, yet came back and proved themselves worthy of greatness later on. Peter was the disciple whom The Man from Nazareth had named as the Rock and yet who denied his master three times, an - experience which did not prevent him from becoming the first leader of the early Christian church.

In the early days of the Second World War, General Sir Neil Ritchie of The Black Watch was relieved of his command by Sir Winston Churchill. He returned to become General Officer Commanding, The Scottish Division, in which capacity he not only achieved great military success but also earned the utter admiration of all those in his command for the manner in which he bravely and resolutely turned personal failure into later success.

There can be few better examples of how a series of abject failures can ultimately result in true greatness than this famous description of Abraham Lincoln:

He failed in business in '31.
He was defeated for State Legislature in '32.
He tried another business in '33. It failed.
His fiancée died in '35.
He had a nervous breakdown in '36.
In '43 he ran for Congress and was defeated.
He tried again in '48 and was defeated again.
He tried running for the Senate in '55. He lost.
The next year he ran for Vice President and lost.
In '59 he ran for the Senate again and was defeated.
In 1860, the man who signed his name A. Lincoln was
elected the 16th President of the United States.
The difference between history's boldest accomplishments,
and its most staggering failures is often,
simply, the diligent will to persevere.

THE PETER PRINCIPLE

Those who abuse or misuse power are often those for whom what is called the Peter Principle has kicked in. What this means is that some people, when promoted beyond their abilities, behave in an over-confident, arrogant or heavy-handed manner to cover up the fact that they are actually not confident at all about coping with the job. In this situation people tend to interfere too much and collapse the tent.

Those in authority may assume that someone who is

brilliant at one job will be equally good at the next job up the ladder. Yet this may well not be the case. Does a good newspaper journalist make a good editor? Not necessarily, because the requirements of the two jobs are very different. When you are catapulted into a job which presents whole new areas of responsibility, it can prove to be a mistake. The journalist who becomes an editor may find that he or she misses doing what they do best – reporting and writing. As an editor they are required to deal with personnel decisions, budgets, advertisers and many other areas which are largely new to them.

Look around you at work and you may find that, either in your own case or perhaps in that of colleagues, the Peter Principle has kicked in. However, it does not always mean that the person in question has been promoted beyond his or natural level of competence. It may simply be a case of getting used to a new job and learning the ropes. This is a time for going forward with caution, self-appraisal and the willingness to learn.

The head of a major public company became notorious for his vanity and self-interest. His preening, self-congratulatory manner was tolerated but not admired by those around him, as was his habit of surrounding himself with admiring young female acolytes. When his company ran into trouble this man failed to see the seriousness of what was happening – he was so self-important that he simply could not see clearly. He continued to play games and to ignore the danger signs, until the day came when he was suddenly removed from power by a board desperate to save the company he had led into crisis. It was only much later that this man, now without a job and the perks he had so coveted, began to see where he had gone wrong.

ARE YOU READY FOR POWER?

How do you know whether you are up to the challenges which power brings? How do you know whether you are a leader in the making, or are better placed in a position in which you respond to authority rather than exercising it?

Not everyone can lead. Not everyone, indeed, even wants to lead or to have power. Leading brings perks, but it also brings enormous pressures; many people would rather not have to cope with these, have no interest in leading, or know instinctively that such a life is not for them.

Others feel drawn to the challenges and responsibilities of leading and see the acquisition of power, with all that it entails, as a major goal in their lives. It isn't always possible to see who will make a good leader and who won't. Despite the fact that there are strong indicators in a potential leader, such as the ability to think clearly, to act with confidence or to display calm resolve under pressure, as well as specific qualities such as presence, poise and style, these are not always enough to make an accurate prediction. Some people come from behind to win a race, just as some who seem to lack leadership potential to start with ultimately come through as fine and upstanding leaders.

If you are interested in acquiring a position in which you can exercise power and authority over others, or you have it already, the following questions will be useful. They will help you to clarify why you want to lead and whether leading is the ideal course for you to pursue, although of course they will not give you a conclusive answer.

- Are you prepared to take the final decision after a group discussion?
- Are you prepared to answer to a client for a mistake that someone else further down the line has made?
- Are you stimulated and energised by decision-making?

the Spirit of Success

- Can you face, calmly and with clarity, a difficult disciplinary task such as firing someone who may have a young family to support?
- Do you look for the potential in everyone, and encourage it?
- Do you feel comfortable with the idea of power, and the spotlight that will be turned on you?
- Do you see the perks and privileges as secondary to the responsibilities of a leadership position?
- Are you prepared to do anything you would ask another person to do?
- Do you want to use a position of power to benefit others, both within and outside your company or community?
- Can you keep a sense of humility, no matter how great the power you have?

You may not know for certain the answers to all these questions. But if you take your time and answer with thoughtfulness and honesty you may achieve a clear picture of whether leadership is right for you or not.

EXERCISE: LEFT ROAD OR RIGHT ROAD?

Decision-making, and standing by your decisions once you have made them, plays a major role in leadership.

Ask yourself how often, when facing decisions, you take the left road and how often the right road. This is a useful exercise for would-be leaders as well as for those already in leadership positions.

The Left Road

This is the road which initially appears most attractive. You know you can find reasons to justify choosing it and that it will lead to some benefits and positive results. But this road is the short-term one, the one which has all the gloss and show but which will not last. If you think clearly and honestly you will know that this road is likely to peter out in disarray, disappointment or destruction. When you choose the left road it is because you want immediate kudos rather than long-term stability and success.

The Right Road

Choosing the right road, the tougher road, may be more difficult in the earlier stages. It appears unattractive, hard-going and demanding. This, however, is the road which truly tests character and which will ultimately bring genuine and lasting rewards. When you choose this road you are going for long-term benefits and are prepared to bypass the glamour of the moment and go for hard work and perseverance.

Making the Right Choice

How often have you picked the left road, telling yourself that it is actually the right one? Choosing the left road is like putting a plaster over a wound without taking the trouble to clean it first. It may seem fine for a while, but in the end it will become infected.

Are you ready to make right-road decisions? To make tough choices which won't win you short-term popularity but which are sound and built on much more solid ground? If so, you have the key hallmarks of a potential leader.

> The story of the US giant Enron is a perfect example of left-road think-ing. The board took the decision to accept a short-term deal with quick profits for themselves and not to disclose the full accounts to shareholders. The auditors acquiesced and were themselves then implicated. As a result of this greed and dishonesty, sixty thousand people lost their livelihoods and pensions. What would the right-road decision have been? To keep things totally honest and to consider the long-term implications of any deal, with the welfare of the employees uppermost in their minds.

THE LEADERSHIP MOMENT

This is the point at which someone who is given power and authority realises the level of responsibility which is inherent in such power and rises to the challenge it presents. If you choose to lead, you will undoubtedly face a leadership moment within a short time of taking up your new position. It may take the form of a realisation, a decision, a brave stand or a bold move forward. For some the leadership moment dawns gradually, while for others it is a single, highly charged and potentially life-changing point in time.

When you have experienced the leadership moment, you know that you are capable of handling the power you have been given. For all true leaders there is a primary leadership moment which defines the course of their leadership and which they never forget. Other leadership moments will follow, and throughout their time in power a leader will face the challenge of such moments. But the first is invariably the greatest test of mettle and strength of character.

> The new chairman of an international aid organisation quickly spotted that there was a major disparity between the salary of the chief executive and those of the other members of the executive team. The CEO had a massive remunerations package which was out of all proportion, not only to that of the rest of his team, but to that of those at his level in similar organisations. He had dug his head into the sand and couldn't see that hanging on to his pay and perks was damaging his organisation and himself in the eyes of others.
>
> The new chairman commissioned an independent inquiry, and in response the CEO began to lobby other board members for their support. This caused even more damage, not least to the trust between himself and other board members.
>
> At last, though, the CEO faced a moment of truth and recognised that the benefits he was taking, including a car allowance and an expense account, were simply not in keeping with the status of his job. He found

the grace and courage to relinquish the benefits package and to institute instead a relatively simple bonus scheme which all could benefit from. The result was that trust was restored and he was seen to have set a marvellous example. The CEO and the chairman built a strong bond and together made the organisation pre-eminent in its field. In fact it is widely regarded as a standard-setter in most external and internal operations and spheres of influence.

At the point when he announced that he would give up the benefits package, this chief executive experienced for the first time in his life a deep and genuine leadership moment. He had been very effective and efficient in all his tasks and duties. He loved the high regard in which he had been held by his colleagues, alongside the opportunity to be a representative 'star' of his organisation in external functions and activities. But these aspects of his job had become so all-consuming that he had lost touch with what it means to be a thoroughly responsible leader. Fortunately he was able to find a deeper wisdom. By addressing his situation in an open, honest and humble way he set a standard for the future, both for himself and for his organisation.

American baseball has a wonderful expression, 'stepping up to the plate', which describes the moment you begin your innings on behalf of your team. It can, of course, be a short-lived experience. Perhaps this explains the electric moment of inner tension and outer excitement in a baseball game when a new player steps up to the plate. A leadership moment, when you step up to the task in hand, is comparable, bringing similar feelings of tension and excitement. A further example might be at the podium or on a stage, when the lights go down and you are the only person at the microphone and the audience is out there waiting for you to begin.

A famous university discovered through one of its board members that the principal was about to be accused of inappropriate conduct. Meetings of university court members were hastily convened, and a full and frank statement from the principal indicated that the facts and circumstances were by no means easy to refute or defend. The reputation of the university was on the line. Both staff and students began to ask searching questions, and the external publicity threatened to become damaging. Interim arrangements were made to replace the principal and his deputy, and all the while the chair and the university court keenly sensed their responsibilities not merely to the present but to the future wellbeing of the university.

The leadership moment came suddenly to some and gradually to others. Amid the chaos and criticism the chair and board had to begin again – to assess the most sensitive way of dealing with the departing principal and his deputy and of finding the best possible leader for the future. The board responded to the clarity and courage of the chair's leadership, to the extent that the unity and efficiency of university court members within meetings and outside them became almost tangible. It was as if the stormy experience was bringing them together – people who have shared a difficult or testing or dangerous experience often sense a feeling of loyalty and camaraderie.

The period of recovery and renewal lasted perhaps three years, after which the chair admitted that it had been the most difficult period of his working life. Yet in many ways it had also been the most challenging and ultimately satisfying, because he and his colleagues had learned so many lessons along the way.

Every member of that particular university court would have gladly volunteered to be somewhere else when the storm clouds broke. Yet in an equivalent way every member would recognise in retrospect the 'leadership moment' when it arrived – when each and every one of them had to choose whether to 'step up to the plate'.

When the victorious British Lions rugby team returned from battling with the All Blacks in New Zealand in 1972, Cambridge University was fortunate to secure the services of the all-conquering Wales and Lions' captain, John Dawes. I was a student at the university then, and a member of the rugby team. John's coaching methodology, based on that of the incomparable Lions' coach Dr Carwyn James, inspired us to new heights. The

> All Blacks were coming to Britain that winter, and were due to play Cambridge in a warm-up Wednesday fixture before their International against Wales at Cardiff the following Saturday. For all of us students, even though there were a number of international players in our XV, this had to be the game of our lives thus far.
>
> John Dawes gathered all his players in the university dressing room after training on the Monday and Tuesday afternoons. There was complete silence on each occasion as he quietly closed the dressing room door. He then walked around the dressing room for some time without saying a word. The silence prevailed until suddenly John turned on his heel and said, 'If any of you has the slightest doubt about playing against the All Blacks, there is the door and now is the time for you to go.' The atmosphere was electric, and similar to that which I experienced later whilst waiting to load up and fly to a dropping zone in order to jump as a member of The Parachute Regiment.
>
> What our coach was doing was giving a perfect demonstration of a leadership moment. His timing, manner and choice of words enabled all the Cambridge players to unite with absolute conviction for the task which lay ahead. The game itself was the most challenging and bruising of our lives so far – but also the most memorable and satisfying.

The leadership moment is the one which brings out the best, not only in the leader but in those around him or her as well. Men and women throughout history have been drawn to examples of courageous and forward-thinking leaders who faced their leadership moments by stepping up to the plate with energy, inspiration and determination. No wonder the actor Russell Crowe's Oscar-winning role as Maximus in the film *Gladiator* has drawn such world-wide acclaim. Witness similar reaction to Mel Gibson as William Wallace in the film *Braveheart* and to Liam Neeson as Rob Roy himself.

It took the extraordinary courage and self-sacrifice of the young nurse, Florence Nightingale, to alert the authorities to the atrocious conditions of the Crimean War in the mid-nineteenth century and as a result she is to this day acknowledged as the founder of the nursing profession as we know it.

It was no surprise that Sir Winston Churchill, on account of his leadership throughout the perilous days of the Second World War, was voted the greatest Briton of the millennium by members of the public. And in this new millennium, is there a more popular and better loved world figure than the first black President of the Republic of South Africa, Nelson Mandela? So courageous and forward-thinking have all these leaders been in stepping up to the plate that history has literally been changed through their leadership moment. Those who are placed in a leadership position today, in whatever capacity and at whatever level, would do well to follow these earlier examples of integrity and perseverance.

VISION AND MISSION

To reach your goals as a leader and then surpass them, to provide clear direction for others and to persevere when the going gets tough, you need a vision of where you are going and a mission which must be fulfilled. In earlier times leadership was often described in terms of heroes: those who did brave and good things, who set up movements and missions amongst mankind and to whom monuments were later built. But that style is not in keeping with the way true contemporary leadership is defined. For instance, many great leaders of previous times so personalised their vision and mission that today their followers would panic and despair at the death of the original founding spirit. In the modern age, true leadership is embodied by the person who is brave and inspired enough to create the vision and the mission and then knows how and when to hand it on. In this way the vision becomes more memorable than the visionary, the ongoing work more vital than the legacy – and, most important of all, the work goes on.

Exercise: the Vision and Mission Test

Take some time away from the hustle and bustle of things, perhaps in a favourite remote or quiet place, to respond to the question: 'What is the vision and mission of my life?' Begin by allowing yourself a maximum of ten sentences and then go away to do something active yet contemplative, such as taking a long walk on your own. When you return some hours later, or even in the freshness of an early morning, try to reduce those ten sentences into perhaps three significant and memorable bullet points. Your ultimate aim will be to have your own personal mission statement of not more than ten words.

The writing of your own vision and mission statement in ten words may sum up what you feel to be your life's purpose, both in your working life and in the wider world. It may also sum up the way you would ultimately like others to view you and to remember you.

FACING RESPONSIBILITY

There are two kinds of responsibility which those in power must face. The first is to yourself and the second is towards others. Both are equally important.

Responsibility Towards Yourself

If you are in a position of power and authority and don't meet your responsibilities towards yourself, you won't be able to meet those you have towards others. This simple truth means that being responsible towards yourself is not self-indulgence but a prerequisite to being a good leader. These self-responsibilities include:

the Spirit of Success

- Being honest with yourself
- Admitting and dealing with your own mistakes
- Taking care of your health and your physical and mental wellbeing
- Keeping your life in balance, so that work is only one, albeit a major, part of it
- Asking for help when you need it
- Recognising your own strengths and weaknesses
- Regularly self-appraising
- Being kind to yourself when you are overtired, ill or under stress
- Making sure you have someone you trust, outside the company, whom you can talk to about your own troubles and pressures
- Making sure that your position means more to you than simply the salary and perks

Responsibility Towards Others

Once you are meeting your responsibilities towards yourself you can begin to be effective in meeting those you have towards others. Those you have authority over will look to you for direction and example. Your responsibilities towards others include:

- Refusing to see yourself as special, chosen or superior, and remembering that no one is indispensable
- Being willing to do yourself anything you ask someone else to do – and demonstrating this
- Sharing the company's success and profits with everyone
- Noticing if someone is down, troubled, ill or overtired, and responding with compassion
- Treating everyone with respect
- Listening to what others have to say
- Enabling others to feel good about their talents and abilities and to enjoy what they do
- Recognising ability in others and passing on responsibility accordingly
- Creating an atmosphere in which working hard is a pleasure

- Encouraging others to have a life outside work and to work reasonable hours

These responsibilities, towards yourself and towards others, are the foundation stones of good leadership and, when met, will bring great rewards in the form of good working relationships, mutual respect, increased productivity and the success of your organisation.

THE EYES HAVE IT

Learning good judgement in choosing and appointing people to roles within your organisation is part of a good leader's responsibility. But how do you know who you can trust and who may turn out to be untrustworthy?

Some time ago I was asked to give the commencement address at a university in the United States. The invitation included the opportunity to give a lecture to the students before they graduated. Following my talk there was a compelling and intelligent question-and-answer session. Towards the end a student rose to ask, 'Mr Drummond, if you had one sentence of advice for us for the rest of our lives, what would it be?' Slightly thrown, I paused, took a deep breath and began to 'busk it' by saying, 'The longer I live, the older I get and the more experienced I become. The more I realise that the bodies which we carry and the outer garments which we wear are mere shells compared to the individuality and special potential of our souls and person-alities. Indeed, it is only when your heart is connected to your head that you can not only feel and be fully alive yourself but also begin to benefit from the innate skills and abilities of perception and intuition already implanted in your soul.'

It was then that the one sentence that had been requested

came to me. 'The eyes have it,' I told them. 'That would be my advice to you and to your fellow graduates for the rest of your lives. For when you look across a table or a room at someone, you may be attracted by them physically or by the brightness or manner of their dress and appearance. But you only really begin to get to know someone, where they are coming from and what their potential might yet be, when you look them in the eyes.'

I have carried this sentence with me ever since, and used it in coaching situations many times. When you meet someone who, rather than looking shifty or glancing away, is willing to look you firmly in the eye, and whose own eyes are clear and confident, you have found someone you can trust and who will let you know where you stand with them. When 'The eyes have it' is used as a guiding principle of intention and intuition, people understand each other better and work for and with each other in more constructive and cooperative ways.

THE BUCK STOPS HERE

Leading can be lonely, as every leader knows and some will admit. As a leader you often have no one above you to give you guidance and direction, to approve or disapprove of what you are doing or to point you in the right direction. Rather, others are looking to you to do this for them, despite the fact that you may not feel certain about the right direction yourself.

It is at times like these that a leader needs strong inner resources. You have to be able to rely on your own judgement and to carry it through, even if you aren't certain that you have chosen the right option. A good leader reviews all the options carefully, and asks advice if it is available. But once the decision is made, whether or not you are certain of its rightness, as a leader you must follow it through with conviction and stand by your decision.

> When I was appointed a headmaster at the age of thirty-two, my long-serving deputy head was double my age at sixty-four! With one year to go to retirement he had offered to see the new head in, and in so many ways he was diligent, thoughtful and courteous to a fault. Yet nothing could have prepared me for the first major disciplinary event of the school year. The deputy head came to see me to explain the rather dire circumstances. As a new Head I began to feel quite vulnerable, so I asked him to sit down in my office so that we could go through things in more detail and find a solution.
>
> 'What shall we do in this situation?' I asked him. 'What would be your advice?' He then outlined two or three alternative options for me. I pressed him further, asking, 'And what would you do?'
>
> With that question he rose swiftly to his feet and said to me, 'That's your decision. I'm off to teach some English.' And with that he left my office. I was left to make the decision alone, which I duly did, and to take in the lesson I had just been given.

That was an experience I have never forgotten, and one which has been extremely useful in my coaching life. I tell this story to people who are taking on a leadership role for the first time, because the harsher realities of the position often take them by surprise. At conferences I often see heads nodding in agreement when I talk about the leadership moment. The first time you are confronted with a 'buck stops here' situation is the moment when you realise that it really is up to you. And at that moment you may feel a degree of loneliness and vulnerability that you have never experienced before.

It is then that character and values begin to play their part, and self-knowledge and self-reliance come to the fore. If you are familiar with self-appraisal – if you have asked yourself who you are, why you are living and working in the way that you are, and what you want to do in the future

– you will be able to rise to the challenge. You will be able to accept your fears and doubts as part of being human, and to go ahead with confidence in yourself and do whatever you have to do.

LOOK BENEATH THE SURFACE

A good leader never accepts what is presented at its face value, but takes the time and trouble to look beneath the surface and establish the true 'warts and all' picture. You can't deal with what is presented in a meeting if you don't know how the position was reached, what people really think, and who is working with – or refusing to work with – anyone else.

I learned this in my early days as the BBC National Governor for Scotland. I used to fly down to London from our home on the Isle of Skye for the monthly Governors' meetings, and it took me some time to understand how they worked. So often I would be presented with the end product of a negotiation or piece of business, which puzzled me. Then I began to realise that all the real work, communication and negotiation had gone on in advance. After a while I started to fly down to London a day early and to spend that extra day finding out what was really going on behind the scenes. I would go to see BBC department heads and find out what the issues were and where the problems lay. In this way I was able to make a bigger contribution and to get more involved in the decision-making. Taking a little time and trouble to sound people out and hear what's going on can make an enormous difference to the outcome.

TRUST YOURSELF

The attraction of power is enormous and many people have pursued it. There is nothing wrong with wanting power, as long as you are sure that you can handle the responsibility which is the key part of the package.

If you have done the necessary work to know who you are and to understand your own strengths and weaknesses, you will know whether you can handle power. If so, you will be the person who has the courage to handle difficulties, to ask for help and to share success.

Working as a member of a team is vital. You may be the team leader, but every member counts and needs to know that they count. The team leader can't do every job or be conversant with every area of expertise, so a good team leader delegates to others when their knowledge and experience are called for. To have the courage to admit that you don't know it all is the hallmark of someone who knows and trusts themselves.

Wise leaders concentrate on what can be changed and improved, and waste very little time or energy on what can't be done. They use their time effectively, and understand that the only justification for holding power is to benefit others.

chapter 9

Keep It Simple

*t*The power of keeping things simple cannot be underestimated, and it is always the simplest way of doing things that is the most effective. Yet all too often we over-complicate matters through paperwork, bureaucracy and endless meetings, with the result that we feel harassed, frustrated, bored and overworked. Fortunately there is absolutely no need to complicate things, and simplifying them is less problematical than most of us imagine. Keeping things simple means developing the ability to see right to the heart of any issue and to deal with it in a direct, brief and sensitive way. This chapter will be about learning to look beyond long-drawn-out decision-making and complicated goals to find the shortest, clearest, simplest path to the desired outcome.

Keeping it simple is one of the most important principles of looking inside to improve what is going on outside. When we look inwards and know ourselves, life instantly becomes simpler. Decisions are made more easily, we are clearer about our goals, and we find it easier to speak and live our truths. Most of my clients, particularly in the public sector and increasingly in the private sector, suffer because their creativity is stifled and sometimes even erased by weighty processes and unnecessary bureaucracy. A lot of the work I do with them is aimed at streamlining and simplifying their working lives, which brings them immense relief.

> A celebrated preacher was in full flow during a packed Sunday morning service when a note was brought to him from his wife, who was in the congregation. The note simply read, 'KISS'. The preacher was delighted by this tender display of affection and encouragement on his wife's part, and felt inspired to make his sermon even longer and more eloquent than usual. For some time he eulogised about the many faces of love, as his audience struggled to keep their attention from straying and their eyes from closing.
>
> When he had finished he went off to find his wife, eager to learn what she had thought of his sermon. 'Didn't you get my note?' she asked him, to which he replied, 'I did – and thank you so much, darling, it's wonderful to know that you care.' Quick as a flash came the response: 'I care so much that I sent the note to remind you to Keep It Simple, Stupid!'

Though it might have dented the ego of the enthusiastic preacher, Keep It Simple Stupid was good advice that we might all remember to take in almost any situation.

Are you in danger of drowning in your own red tape? Do you feel wedded to your endless 'to do' list? Does your adrenalin rush have more to do with the complications of life than with too much caffeine? If so, it's time to learn to simplify and to save your health and sanity at the same time.

If you feel that your life has become needlessly, yet unavoidably, complicated, you are not alone. The emphasis on process and bureaucracy has become almost epidemic on both sides of the Atlantic and nowhere is this more apparent than in the public sector, particularly in relation to local or national government. Endless repetition, needless complexity and tiers of decision-makers have left many of those who work in this sector ready to pull their hair out. If a straw poll of executives was to be taken throughout the United States and the United Kingdom, top of the list of their troubles would be the distracting and de-energising weight and force of process and bureaucracy.

As Charles Handy, the internationally acclaimed management guru and author, has said, 'We are all running harder to stay in the same place.' In one lecture he talked about the modern world's 'need' for material goods which is symptomatic of the way we have overcomplicated life:

> Chindogu is a Japanese word for unnecessary things. My favourite example is windscreen wipers for your spectacles which come on when you go out in the rain. But chindogu can be less exotic. I have far more ties than I will ever need, or books that I will never read. Our shopping malls are full of chindogu – nothing that you really need. Christmas has become a chindogu festival.
>
> As I grow older I find that retail therapy no longer appeals. I don't need or want more stuff. How do you put a monetary measure on the air we all use? What about beauty, or quiet streets, or what Adam Smith, the Scottish moral philosopher, called cultivation? W. Edwards Deming, the man who taught the Japanese to value quality, used to say that 90 per cent of the things that matter in organisations can't be counted.

This last point is particularly important. The more 'things' you have, beyond what is actually needed, the harder it is to keep life simple. This is as true for organisations as it is for individuals. The more meetings, files, referrals, reports, agendas and general paperwork, the harder it is to produce clear, simple results. Keeping it simple means clearing away the excess, the distractions, the meaningless rules and pointless rituals, and paring back to what really counts and makes a difference.

BLAME CULTURE

So why do organisations overcomplicate things in this way? The primary reason is that so many people at the top have lost confidence in themselves – in who they are and in what they bring to that particular position. Fear of what others might think and of the knock-on effect of even the smallest action has led to paralysis. Things happen at snail's pace, if at all, because they have to go through a complex system of checks and balances in which they are approved, copied to a dozen departments, rubber-stamped and reapproved.

We live in a culture of complaint and blame, and this is the source of the complications which are leading to virtual standstill. Too many people are afraid of being blamed, sued or otherwise found at fault. This fear is killing off initiative, leadership, decisiveness and forward-thinking and replacing these qualities with caution, overchecking, buck passing and evasion.

For instance the chair of a public inquiry, or the head of what is referred to in the United Kingdom as a quango (quasi-autonomous non-governmental organisation), may be inclined towards a radical decision or viewpoint. In the pioneering days, with less red tape and bureaucracy, that chair might have felt able to follow through with such a decision, which might then have resulted in a simple and far-reaching solution. Yet across our institutions, universities, churches, hospitals and so forth, the fear of negative consequences and blame has led to the avoidance of such clear and radical decisions. Instead another committee is set up, which produces yet more paperwork (mostly unread) to verify that what was proposed earlier was sensible, or, even worse, to confirm that the doubters could have been right and to postpone action. This increasingly common tendency to relegate decisions to yet another committee, to yet another policy paper and to further inaction and indecision, can assume almost life- or career-threatening proportions.

STAND BACK

Many of the clients I see are people who have been virtually brought to their knees by the sea of red tape which surrounds them. Struggling with it has demoralised and exhausted them. Instead of using their considerable skills to benefit the organisation they work for, they spend increasing amounts of time ploughing through piles of paperwork and chasing others for decisions.

It is no wonder, then, that so many men and women in responsible positions value the opportunity to 'come apart' for a while in the quietness of a one-to-one confidential coaching session. Not only are they able to put aside the hustle and bustle of normal circumstances, they are also able to talk in complete confidence about the pressures they feel. This opportunity to step aside from the fray allows them to find a new perspective and to feel stronger and clearer about the way forward.

A Swiss client felt that after a handful of coaching sessions he had begun to use what he termed his 'inside muscles'. He explained that he felt much more 'in the flow of life' and able to live in and with the present moment, rather than always endeavouring to change the people and circumstances around him. Such acceptance of what you cannot change is a key to finding simplicity. The energy and effort which might have been wasted on trying to force impossible changes can then be used to make constructive and forward-thinking changes in those areas where change is possible.

What coaching can do is help a client to stand back from the overwhelming demands of his or her workplace and see the bigger, clearer picture. This is vital for making effective, lasting and positive changes.

A leading property developer with great entrepreneurial spirit and whose judgement was well respected felt overwhelmed by the frustration of dealing with minor officials. Time after time these petty bureaucrats demanded that he go back to the drawing board for yet another report or still more alterations. He could not continue to live and work like this, and feared for his own future and that of his many employees across the country. How, he asked, could he develop a new approach and so learn to live with and work around such weighty bureaucracy?

We decided to go for a Keep It Simple strategy. He enjoyed a game of golf, and this seemed like a good place to start. What is the basic principle of successful and accurate golf? Keep your swing simple.

And so our property developer went back to his drawing board. He worked out where and when and how and with whom things were 'swinging' simply and well. He then concentrated on these areas, letting several of his more obstructive and wearying clients go. He also cut back on his firm's paperwork, insisting that no document or report be longer than six sides of A4 paper and that lengthy paragraphs be condensed to bullet points, while important points were to be highlighted. Every member of his organisation was then trained to operate in the most simple and effective way, by giving clear, brief information without superfluous paperwork or analysis.

From this time forward the property developer began to enjoy his work again, and found that he was increasingly attracting the kind of clients who also enjoyed working in a simple and straightforward way.

What this property developer did was to stand back from the frustration of his job and see where he could make a difference. What I suggested to him, and have suggested to many others, was the Friday Rule. This simple technique has been enthusiastically taken up by a number of companies, who now encourage not only the top executives but all the other workers to follow it.

THE FRIDAY RULE

The Friday Rule simply states: Take one Friday afternoon a month off and spend it sitting in a café or some other peaceful spot, with a cup of coffee and a pen and paper in front of you. Use this time, away from the hurly-burly of work, to assess how things are going. What needs addressing? What needs changing? Who needs encouraging? What's working and what's not working? Take your time, allow your thoughts to wander a little, slow down and enjoy your coffee. Use this as a time for clear, unhurried vision, for enjoyment and for recognising your priorities.

The STARBUCKS Test

What better test to give yourself over your coffee than this one? I use this as an aid to the Friday Rule and encourage clients to try it as a means of organising and sorting their thoughts.

STA = STAndards

Are you setting the right standards for your organisation? Are those standards ones you can be proud of? Where could things be clarified or improved? Does everyone in the organisation understand what the standards are and work by them? There's no point in having standards if they are not kept.

R = Review

How's it all going? When was the last time you received honest feedback, or gave yourself a self-appraisal session? What do you feel pleased with in your personal progress and in your organisation? What worries you and what can you do about it?

163

B = no Blame

Has laying blame become part of the culture in your organisation? What or who is suffering because of this? Do you tend to lay blame rather than taking responsibility? How can you turn things around?

C = Courage

What issues need to be addressed? What's getting in the way, and where can calm and thoughtful leadership intervention help to make things better? Do you have the courage of your convictions? Are you courageous in setting an example for others?

KS = Kick Ass and Kindness

Both are needed at different times. How well do you keep the balance between the two? Are you using them in appropriate ways, or do you veer more strongly towards one than the other? Do you know how to kick ass just enough to encourage without demoralising? Do you know when kindness can make all the difference?

U = You

This one is deliberately left until last. Where and how can you influence things for the better both at work and at home? What's going on for you right now in your life? When did you last review your personal vision and mission for the wholeness of your own life? Does this still fit with the corporate mission statement and energy and impetus of the organisation which you are working for or leading?

Opting in, Not Opting Out

The Friday Rule, incorporating the STARBUCKS Test, is an effective way of simplifying life by standing back from it on a regular basis. Don't make the mistake of thinking it's an opt-out. In fact the reverse is true – it's a way of opting in with more commitment and insight.

Clients who have tried it report fantastic results and increased efficiency. Taking time out to think about how things are going really helps them to keep a clear and far simpler perspective. Many creative and imaginative managers and leaders have insisted that staff in their departments make the Friday Rule part of their working lives.

After the café session and the STARBUCKS Test I often suggest to clients that they should forget about work for the rest of the afternoon and do something different like collecting their children from school, playing sports or going for a walk. And at least once a month try to begin your weekend early and be kind to yourself and to those who live with you and care for you. In this way the Friday Rule helps to recharge your batteries, so that you can return to work on Monday with a much fresher and clearer mind-set.

Anne had been appointed head of a think-tank within a government department. She was delighted with her new role and approached it with enthusiasm and energy, hoping that the think-tank would be able to make far-reaching recommendations which might eventually change the law in this particular area. However, after four months in the job Anne was finding the amount of red tape she had to deal with stifling and infuriating. She felt that trying to make progress was like trying to move through a thick fog – tricky at best. On top of this there was a lot of backbiting and gossip, so the atmosphere was tense.

Anne began using the Friday Rule to give herself a little space and distance from everything that was going on at work. She found that after an hour walking by the river in her local park, and another hour sitting over her coffee in a quiet café, she felt human again. She was also able to put together some ideas for change, before going to collect her young daughter from school and spending a fun evening together.

Over the next few months Anne made gradual changes, based on her Friday afternoon decisions. She moved the worst gossips and encouraged

> those who showed promise. She also asked those who needed a decision to come straight to her, instead of going through the bureaucratic jungle, and encouraged her staff to talk to one another rather than writing endless memos, emails and reports. The result was that Anne's enthusiasm for her job returned and the think-tank was able to come up with a truly excellent set of recommendations.

STREAMLINING

If you want to keep things simple your organisation, however large or small, will almost certainly benefit from a little streamlining. All this means is cutting back on waste, whether that means time, paper or energy. Here are my ten tips for streamlining your operation.

1. Be Well Organised

This is the first rule of keeping things simple. A well-organised workspace means you can put your hands on whatever you need with minimum time and effort. It is amazing how often businesses and organisations of whatever size lack the basics for keeping life simple, such as clearly labelled files, drawers and cupboards. In addition, a well-organised diary enables you to know where you need to be at any given time, and ensures that you have enough time for appointments and between them. If you are well organised in your life, you are likely to be well organised in your thinking too.

2. Cut Down on Paperwork

A short, clear and to-the-point document is far more effective than a huge, long-winded one. Like our friend the property developer, try setting a maximum length for reports and other documents. Encourage staff to cut back on point-less communications, too.

3. Send Fewer Emails

The advent of email has failed to reduce travel or phone bills, and has actually increased our workload. So often emails simply use time and effort for very little genuine productivity or value, especially as a person who receives 150 a day (as so many people do) tends to take very little notice of them. Often a quick word in person is far more effective.

4. Cut Down on Journeys

Very often, because of frenetic activity leading to poor planning, three or four trips are undertaken to a particular location when, with calm and thoughtful planning, a single journey could well have been enough. This kind of excess travel benefits only the airlines.

5. Cut Down on Meetings

Nothing consumes more time in the workplace than unnecessary meetings. The chairman of a private investment company, feeling overwhelmed by demands, took his coach's advice and agreed to attend only those meetings where he was genuinely needed. A glance at his diary revealed that the previous week he had attended over thirty meetings within and outside the office. But on the basis of his new agreement, the following week he attended only five meetings, each of which was enjoyable and successful.

6. Discourage Gossip

Why? Because gossip is not only destructive and hurtful, creating a bad atmosphere in any workplace, but it is also enormously time-consuming. Gossip adds unnecessary complications. A little effort put into fostering good relations between staff, and a clear message that gossip is not acceptable, may reap rewards in both enthusiasm and productivity.

7. Undertake Regular Clear-Outs

Spring-cleaning, at any time of year, creates fresh space and fresh energy. Throwing out everything you don't need is both practical and symbolic, because getting rid of the old always makes way for the new. Paperwork, in particular, can mount up as documents are stored away as a precaution and then forgotten for months or years. Set a time, once a year, when you and those around you will clear out the old. Apply this also to outdated practices and ideas. What are you holding on to that is no longer really useful?

8. Have Well-defined Goals

If you know where you are heading, you can put your energy into how to get there. If you don't have clear goals and aims, your energy is likely to be spread too far and wide and will be wasted in certain areas. Choose your goals and decide when you want to achieve them. Don't have too many – three or four is more than enough. Subdivide goals into achievable segments, and update them regularly by reviewing progress.

9. Make Clear Decisions

Nothing is more stress-inducing than putting off a difficult decision which must be made. Get into the habit of making decisions after a reasonable, but not excessive, amount of time, during which you weigh up the options. Life and work are full of decisions, and some of them are going to be tough ones. Even after a decision is made you may not feel certain it is the right one. Better, though, to make a decision, even a wrong one, than to hesitate indefinitely. And once you have decided, put your doubts aside and throw your energy and effort into making the decision work.

10. Remember That Less is More

This is the golden rule for keeping things simple. Often a brief note is more effective than a long letter, a short speech more powerful than a long one, a phone call more constructive than a long email. If you keep this in mind in all your dealings and decisions, you will make your working life much simpler. Cut to the point, focus on what really matters and let all the excess go.

A senior executive of a large bank came for coaching because he felt his life was consumed by demands. He worked very hard but felt he got comparatively little done, though he was unsure why this was so. When we looked at how he spent his working week it certainly seemed full. There were a huge number of meetings and appointments as well as evenings working late to catch up with paperwork, which he then took home as well.

I suggested that together we apply some of the rules of simplicity to his working life. As he went through them he realised that he was dealing with a lot of inefficiency and excess paperwork. Added to which, he would often spend several minutes at a time searching for documents he needed.

Fired with enthusiasm, he began to make changes. He asked his personal assistant to set up a clear filing system so that he could access the documents he needed at a moment's notice. He then dramatically reduced the length of any reports and memos he wrote. He also cut back on emails and meetings. He selected three priority goals for the next month and directed his efforts towards them, setting aside other demands which were simply distractions.

A month on, he looked like a different man. The haggard, frowning person who first arrived had been replaced by a smiling, far more relaxed version. Simplifying his way of operating, he told me, had taken years off him and enabled him to enjoy his job for the first time in years.

DEAL WITH TODAY

One of the most important aspects of keeping things simple is learning to deal with what is going on right now, rather than worrying about what might happen in the future. Many people spend the vast majority of their time thinking about the past and the future, often to the extent that they hardly notice the present at all. This is a shame, since the past can't be changed and the future can't be known. The present is all we have.

This is as true in business as in any other area of life. Today's deal, negotiation, meeting or exchange is what counts. Put your focus on that and your efforts into making it the best it can be. When you do this, the future tends to take care of itself.

Of course, planning is important – and careful planning will determine certain aspects of the future. What isn't useful is needless worrying about things which might never happen. Things are just as likely to go right as they are to go wrong, so why not deal with the present and trust that the future will work out? Keeping it simple involves the ability to prioritise, to know what really matters and to focus on what needs to be done right now.

We are all experts at overcomplicating life. We know how to juggle, to worry about six things at once, to be in several places almost simultaneously and to cram just one more thing into an already overfull day. Making the decision to keep things simple brings a great deal of relief. Simplifying your environment, your structures and your days allows you the room to think and act creatively, to decide what really matters and to achieve your goals.

chapter 10

Make a Difference

*N*o matter how great your success in the work-place, there comes a time when it is necessary to ask your-self whether you have made a real, visible and positive difference to the lives of others. To make a difference doesn't just mean being the person who got the biggest sales record for the month or who got promoted in double quick time. It means looking beyond your immediate environment to the world outside, seeing what needs doing and who needs help and then taking action. It means self-involvement and the encouragement of others at work in projects within and outside daily business, in order to benefit those least able to help themselves.

In this chapter I want to look at what it means to make a real difference in the lives of others, and why it is so vital that we all aim to do this. I believe that each one of us has a responsibility, both individually and with others, to help, encourage and support those who are in need. This is not the same as charitable giving. While giving to charity – and some organisations are enormously generous – is highly creditable, what I am talking about is social responsibility.

Very often the chair or chief executive of a leading company sees its corporate duty to others, having made the profit required, as a charitable contribution. Hence the prevalence of company foundations and major charitable drives, all of which do fine and generally very constructive work in their own ways. There is, however, something more. There is personal involvement. The willingness to give time, effort, energy, expertise, advice and encouragement on a regular, committed basis.

Many work-driven people whose lives revolve around long hours, profits, analysis and rocketing up the company ladder may hold their hands up in horror and say, 'Great idea, but I haven't got a minute to spare. My life is crammed full with work, my family and social activities. How can I possibly fit in anything else?' I would argue, though, that the 'something else' is not an optional extra but a vital ingredient in a truly rounded, fulfilled and successful life. Success without contribution is hollow and ultimately unsatisfying. The greater the power you hold, the more necessary it is to recognise the importance of giving to and serving others. Many great leaders have acknowledged the simple truth that to lead is to serve. Any other route leads, inevitably, towards abuse of power.

During the Queen's Golden Jubilee celebrations a sixty-five-year-old lady from Glasgow recalled hearing the then Princess Elizabeth's twenty-first birthday radio broadcast. The words which she heard and remembered for the next fifty years were: 'I declare this day that I dedicate my life, whether long or short, to your service.' 'Those words shaped my outlook on life from that moment onwards,' the woman said. The Queen has been true to her word, and in so doing has set a powerful example. To serve others, in whatever respect, is to give generously of yourself – the greatest gift you have to offer.

When the young Hector Laing returned from the Second World War in 1946, after service as a tank troop commander with the Scots Guards, he was keen to get involved with the family business, McVitie's of Robertson Avenue in Edinburgh. Hector arrived at work early the first morning, before the first shift, as he was to continue to do throughout his long business career. When the first shift came to work he made his way amongst the biscuit makers, sat down beside an elderly worker, introduced himself and asked how he enjoyed working at McVitie's Robertson Avenue. The old man turned to Hector and said, 'Well, Mr Laing, do ye ken Peterhead Jail?' To which the eager, fresh-faced young man replied, 'Yes, but not intimately!' The old man then went on, 'Well, Mr Laing, the only difference between McVitie's Robertson Avenue and Peterhead Jail is that at McVitie's ye get oot for yer dinner!'

Excited about this obvious potential for improvement, Hector set about transforming the place and bringing into the company the sense of commitment and ownership which he had experienced in the tanks in wartime. In the end he achieved this and much, much more. Within a few years McVitie's became part of the much larger, successful and increasingly respected United Biscuits plc.

Hector, by now Sir Hector and later to become Lord Laing of Dunphail, convened his final annual general meeting in the Assembly Rooms at George Street in Edinburgh in the summer of 1986, after forty years' unbroken service to the company. The shareholders were keen both to congratulate him and praise him on his outstanding business performance over the years. In the question-and-answer session which followed the reading of the main report a grateful shareholder rose to thank him and to ask, 'What plans do you have for your retirement, Sir Hector?' He replied that his plans were many and he had no worries about keeping active and busy. He went on to say that what really worried him, however, was what would happen to him when his time came to face his Creator and to give an account of his life. He imagined St Peter meeting him at the pearly gates and asking, 'And what have you done with your life, Hector Laing?' To which Hector would recount his long and distinguished record of achievement. After which, he explained, he fully expected the reply, 'Very good. But tell me, Hector, what else have you done with your life?'

Sir Hector had, in fact, done much else with his life. Firstly, he had set up the One Per Cent Club, which encouraged major companies to donate 1 per cent of their annual turnover to their local communities. In addition he was instrumental in founding Business in the Community throughout the United Kingdom, thus encouraging a whole wave of companies to be more responsible for social and economic issues in their respective communities. He also managed to persuade HRH The Prince of Wales to become Patron of that distinguished organisation. Yet, being the kind of man he was, he was still uncertain whether his individual contribution had been sufficient. And it was this contribution, he was sure, which would be the one that really counted.

THINKING OUTSIDE THE BOX

Sir Hector's 'what else' is often the trigger for many other questions. When I ask clients what else they feel they have done or might like to do, our conversation often leads back to those three fundamental questions at the start of this book: Who am I? Why am I living and working in the way that I am? What else might I yet do with the rest of my life?

Very often in a one-to-one coaching session I can be sitting opposite a very senior player responsible for the working lives, jobs and futures of thousands. Yet when the 'what else' question arises they begin to muse about how limited or narrow their lives have become. Many corporate executives feel they have lost touch with their background. When this happens, it is time to begin to think 'outside the box'.

This is the phrase I use for moving beyond the self-imposed restrictions of our lives, whatever those restrictions may be. But when you begin to think outside the box, you open yourself up to numerous possibilities of thought and action. This can be enormously stimulating and challenging, and also sometimes a little nerve-racking. If you can move the goalposts in any direction you want, what might this allow you to do? The first step in discovering the answer to this question is to look at what you have to offer and what you might like to do. What lights you up? The TICK test, featured in Chapter 1, can be very useful here to remind you of your talents, abilities and interests.

Visiting a major bank with worldwide connections, I found myself in a cavernous elevator full of people making their way to the fifty floors above. At the canteen/restaurant floor three young staff members entered and began to talk. A male banker, talking loudly across the elevator to a female banker and her companion, began to bait her about another male member of staff. After some minutes the young female banker could take no more. She almost shouted across the packed elevator, 'If you must know, Andrew has been living, breathing, working and smiling alongside me for the past eight months or more, OK?', before stomping out of the elevator.

When I arrived at my destination I could not resist describing my experience to the head of the bank and asking whether this mentality was typical of the culture there. He agreed that it probably was, and told me he was saddened by it.

We had a long and helpful discussion, out of which arose his particular 'what else?' After so many years concentrating almost solely on the bank, this talented and exceptional man has now become personally involved in a number of causes which are close to his heart. He not only donates to

> them but finds the time to visit them regularly and to encourage their progress. Going even further, he has encouraged this kind of generosity throughout the bank, and as a result there has been a marked improvement in the morale and attitude of the staff.

Discovering your own personal 'what else' may take some time, but it is worth the effort. There are countless opportunities to make a difference. I have seen clients achieve a great deal of satisfaction and delight from activities such as giving children football coaching, encouraging teenagers to develop business ideas, and spending a couple of hours a week helping with a local charity. Whether the project you become involved with is small or large, local or national, is unimportant. What matters is that it has meaning to you and that you feel you are making a difference.

Real Work

My own particular opportunity to make a difference has come through the development of the Columba 1400 Leadership Centre on the Isle of Skye. Seeing the young people who have arrived cowed and without a shred of self-belief leaving only days later with their heads high and full of plans for their future is humbling and joy-giving. Many of them have moved from homelessness and poverty into education and work as a result of their leadership academy training. This is what makes the effort worthwhile for all those involved in the teaching and support work.

One of my great inspirations was the late Joe Slovo, the first Minister for Housing in the newly formed South African Government of National Unity in 1994. Joe, a wonderful speaker and storyteller, once said: 'We cannot start off with the approach that any human being is beyond reach.'

Many of my clients want to know more about Columba 1400. Often, at their request, I have shown them a video of the work being undertaken amidst the tough realities of the meanest streets in the United Kingdom and overseas. Inevitably there will be a deep and prolonged silence afterwards, and on occasion misty eyes. Most say something along the lines of, 'Others may think me important, and I may well be responsible for many people and a huge budget, but, in comparison with touching the life of even one other human being in such a deep and meaningful way, all I can say is that what you are involved in is "real work".'

These clients feel there is a fundamental gap between the work they do in the corporate world and the work of making a difference to the lives of others. And many of them feel a deep desire to do some 'real work' and begin to make a difference. Some know exactly what they want to do, but others have no idea where to start.

The best place to begin is usually in your own community. Look around and you will soon find people who can benefit from a little of your time, energy, experience and knowledge. Be prepared to get involved, to notice what is needed and to be hands-on. Clients often report that the sense of heaviness and responsibility which they feel so much of the time lifts and is forgotten when they involve themselves with others in this way. They also find that it helps to improve their work/life balance, and that they soon begin to look forward to this involvement as an oasis of calm in their hectic lives.

The benefits of this 'real work' can spread to all areas of your life. Being a fully rounded and fulfilled person will enable you to run a rounded, fulfilling and worthwhile business or organisation. The benefits work in both ways, and can bring community and business affairs into a mutually responsible and beneficial relationship.

The following is an extract from the Rotary Literacy Champion Award citation made to Naggapan Parasuraman in recognition of his foundation of an all-day school for the poor in Chennai, India. Although he is by no means a wealthy man himself, Parasuraman's 'what else' has realised the dreams of more than 120 children to have an education.

> To become what you are today is outstanding. But to kindle the fire, to share this passion for self-education among your less privileged peers, calls for genius. Starting the cycle for social upliftment by opening a 'thanneer pandal' at a road junction, you took to encouraging children to study. From thatched huts in 1987, when you had not met your mentor, you nurtured your dream of a school for everyone who cannot go to school. By 1995 you had single-handedly constructed a room to house this hope for the hopeless. Today, one of those you cared for is an engineer. Run by a small band of seven friends to help you, you mix with the elite of the international scientific community at work, and by evening, you transform the lives of the world's most economically deprived slum dwellers.
>
> They say, when you open a school you close down a prison. You have closed the prison of ignorance in many minds. You have eliminated many potential criminals by offering them the gift of education.
>
> Your life runs on the vision and actions to make LITERACY a household word. The true key to our national growth is individual empowerment.
>
> You are a champion who has admired success and dreams of sharing it with others. A rare contribution of missionary zeal and passionate pursuit of excellence in education. May the effort continue!

To make a difference in such a profound way is surely one of the most exciting things any of us can do. And every one of us is capable of this. No matter what your circumstances or what stage you have reached in life, you can choose to make a difference.

THE FIVE Ps

At the Sister Cities World Peace Conference in Fort Worth, Texas, which I attended in July 2002, the younger delegates were keen to address the question of how they could make a difference to others. So pressing were their questions and their desire for a working model that I came up with the following exercise. It had certainly been the foundation stone of the success of Columba 1400, and can be applied to any particular project in your own life.

The five Ps stand for:

- People
- Partnerships
- Pioneering
- Persevering
- Prayer

People

When you set out on your 'what else' journey, always look for people whose cups are half-full rather than half-empty. You will, inevitably, encounter people who will tell you that whatever you are aiming to do can't be done. Some will be threatened by your drive and initiative, and may find that your zeal and energy expose something lacking in their own hearts and lives. Don't waste too much time or energy endeavouring to persuade them at this stage, and don't allow yourself to be demoralised by their criticism.

Instead, surround yourself with those who are prepared to think positively, to look for solutions rather than problems, and to believe that the project will be accomplished. The Nike motto, 'Just do it', is an apt one here. In the early stages of a 'what else' adventure you need special people whom you trust and believe in, and who fundamentally trust and believe in you. This was certainly our experience at Columba 1400, where at the outset there was such a feeling of camaraderie, care and wellbeing that nothing was allowed to stand for long against our common purpose. We believed we could do it, and our belief and determination were strong enough to overcome all obstacles. Finding the right people is crucial to the success of your project, as is having the courage to part with those who are not fully supportive.

> I well remember, after an unexpected and disappointing change of personnel, how a certain type of politics and intrigue was introduced into the organisation, much to my shock and dismay. For a while many of us were somewhat unsettled and wondering what had happened to the 'what else' purpose of our project. We had to review the situation fundamentally and radically before we realised that certain crucial decisions had to be faced and made and that we had to part company with those who were undermining the project. Only when we had moved beyond the culture of cynicism, fear and gossip could the 'what else' breathe and begin to flourish again.

Partnerships

Both in the United Kingdom and in the United States, in the not-for-profit sector a whole host of like-minded endeavours are often launched at the same time. Inevitably people have similar ideas, and projects are initiated which have aims and remits in common. The worst aspect is that these organisations may compete against one another for the same pots of public or private funding. This can lead to an unfortunate and misplaced sense of competition which harms the good causes these organisations support.

Avoid this kind of unnecessary and wasteful competition if you can. When you begin your 'what else' project, whether individual or collective, small or large, search for those organisations with whom you can easily begin a strong partnership. Mutual cooperation can often bring about great mutual benefit in the most surprising ways.

Recent research provided by the University of Glasgow for the Lloyds TSB Foundation for Scotland indicated that four charities or not-for-profit organisations were starting up every week. If this is happening in a small country like Scotland, how many must be launched every week in larger countries? Surely the time has come for proactive partnering in order to share the resources, energy and ideas available, rather than squandering them through ill-judged competitiveness. One of Scotland's greatest living social entrepreneurs, John Moorhouse, formerly of Shell UK, former chief executive of Scottish Business in the Community, has a key phrase when it comes to successful and fulfilling partnerships within the not-for-profit sector: 'There is no limit to what we can achieve, so long as we don't mind who gets the credit'.

> At an early stage in our Columba 1400 journey we found ready partners in Sir Tom Farmer, founder of Kwik-Fit, Sir Peter Burt, Governor of the Bank of Scotland and Sir Peter Vardy, Chairman of Reg Vardy, all of whom brought vision, belief and support to the project. Our work also gained support and encouragement from such well-respected organisations as Youth at Risk, the Big Issue in Scotland and the Prince's Trust. Those private and public partnership beginnings gave us the courage and determination to launch the project. Since then we have continued to express our belief in partnership, and as a result many other supporters have come forward in a spirit of good will and purpose.

Pioneering

The one thing that is guaranteed to cross the mind of anyone who is setting out on a pioneering venture, usually at the darkest, toughest moment, is 'What on earth have I got myself into?' In fact, if this thought doesn't cross your mind at least a dozen times during your 'what else' project, either it isn't pioneering or your nerves are made of solid steel!

To translate pioneering thoughts – which come all too easily – into pioneering actions – which are all too rare – is a huge step. And at many points during the process it will feel strange and unfamiliar. To see it through to completion requires real boldness, determination and a point-blank refusal to take no for an answer. But for every block, for every problem or hazard, there is a fresh route, a word of encouragement or a helping hand to be found. Within the heart of the pioneer there is a deep, energising strength which knows that you have to begin somewhere and then build as well as you can, knowing that the stones which you lay will provide secure foundations for those who come after you.

It is often said that 'It is impossible fully to understand another person's furrow until you have ploughed it.' So it is with the pioneer or the prospective pioneer. You will perhaps never fully understand the pioneering process until you have lived it and reached a stage when you can look back and say, 'Well, we made it this far.' And then the pioneering spirit will kick in again and urge you upwards and onwards!

> I well remember standing among the foundations at Columba 1400. We were wearing hard hats, the rain was dripping steadily and we jumped from puddle to puddle as we toured the site. A member of the group then stood looking out of the still windowless building, into the teeth of a gale, and said, 'You know, if I'd been involved in this project from the start, I would never have built it this way'! How helpful, I thought, with the builders already on site. Of course he may have had a point – we might well do many things differently with the freedom which hindsight allows. But a little support at that stage would have gone a long way.

Persevering

In Chapter 7 we looked at the Columban Code of Values – awareness, focus, creativity, integrity, perseverance and service. If the pioneers of Columba 1400 were to be asked which value was most needed during those early days, their answer would undoubtedly be perseverance. In the pioneering country of 'what else', when you strive to make a difference the knock-backs come fast and frequent. Often other people's indifference – or, even worse, their eager anticipation of your failure – will set you back or stop you in your tracks. People will tell you that 'It's never been done before', or that 'The last time it was attempted it failed', or even 'Who are you to be thinking of such an enterprise, particularly at your age and stage?' But if you are willing to persevere, you can move rapidly beyond your detractors and steadfastly towards success.

> During an important BBC dinner for the Broadcasting Council for Scotland in Glasgow, at which I was due to speak, I was called urgently to the phone. A worried voice on the other end said, 'Our builders have gone bust.' We were in the early stages of building Columba 1400, at an anticipated cost of £1.5 million, and our carefully selected building contractors had failed to meet their payments in another part of the country. As a result they were required to go into liquidation, which meant the Columba 1400 site would have to be locked up. There have been few colder showers in my life, and yet I had to return to that dinner to speak and act as if nothing had happened.
>
> Thinking it through later, I began to realise a number of things. Yes, there would be those who would now be queuing for tickets for the memorial service for Columba 1400. Those who over the months and years of planning had reserved the right to be right about our failure and in certain cases were looking forward to that event. For instance, I remembered one member of the local planning committee, having endorsed the outline proposals, saying, 'Remember, no one has ever raised £1 million for such a project on the Isle of Skye.' He had just agreed to something that he was doubting only minutes later.
>
> Then I remembered the other people who were looking to me for an

example and a way forward. Those older people within the community who had been so thrilled and delighted that the younger, up-and-coming generation would benefit from facilities which they had never had when they were young. The people and the partnerships already created were strong and worthwhile, and I think it was then that I decided we weren't going to go down that easily. And so perseverance, perseverance, and perseverance became the order of each and every day.

The blow had cost us dearly, but given time, more fund-raising and careful planning we were able to engage new contractors and get the project up and running again. What kept us going was our determination to see the project come to fruition and not to let down all those people who were willing us to succeed.

Prayer

What happens when, with as many of the right people and partnerships as you can muster, and despite your pioneering and persevering spirit, there are still moments when you feel absolutely stuck? Which of us hasn't experienced a time when we felt debilitated and wondered whether we could honestly go on and rise to the next challenge?

It is in these moments that the power of prayer becomes a wonderful resource. It is when the chips are down and we feel unable to carry on that we feel most alone. At times like this it can help to pray, and to realise that in fact we are not alone. Whatever your religious or spiritual persuasions, the sense that there is a higher power there to share the burden is enormously comforting. When speaking to parents about turbulent adolescent behaviour, a head teacher will often say, 'It is when our young people appear to need us least that they in fact need us most.' It is the same with prayer. When we tell ourselves we don't need it, that it's pointless and can't make a scrap of difference, that is when we have our greatest need of it.

Most of us are good at putting a brave face on things. The world out there may think you are confident and forging ahead, but inwardly you may be knowing the depths of despair and disappointment. It is only when you are alone that you can let down your guard and be honest with yourself. Prayer at such a time is strengthening, enlightening and comforting.

A sanctuary such as Columba 1400, amidst the beautiful mountains and captivating seas of the magical, misty Isle of Skye, provides its own spiritual outlet. There is no better place in which to take time out to be alone with yourself, with nature and with the spirits of those whose presence continues to surround you through life and death.

When the human heart can 'chill and still' (a favourite Columba 1400 expression) it is then that an infinite source of power and strength and comfort can flood into your being, refuel your cylinders and accompany you through the stresses and strains, as well as through the choices and challenges. It is then that you feel carried and accompanied, so that the 'what else' of your life and work begins to realise itself almost without the need for personal influence and control.

What has happened? Vision has predominated over personality, the cause has replaced controversy, trust has overtaken fearfulness and the spiritual has taken over from the everyday.

The lessons learned through the five Ps of People, Partnerships, Pioneering, Persevering and Prayer are ones which will shape and enable you for the rest of your life. These lessons learned along the way and the experiences they bring, however painful and miserable at the time, are those which really shape your character and enable you to discover your true inner potential.

THE BLESSINGS OF DISCOVERING YOUR 'WHAT ELSE'

Those executives who have made the effort to recognise a 'what else' in their lives have found many benefits. The knowledge that their 'what else' is giving help, strength, comfort and encouragement to others is deeply fulfilling. More than this, though, they have escaped the limited and limiting mentality that I came across in the elevator of a large bank and have found width and depth in their lives. Often they have discovered the truth of the Celtic saying I quoted in Chapter 1: 'In order to understand where you are going you have to understand where you come from.' They have rediscovered their roots and background, which have enabled them to move forward more strongly and with greater confidence.

By taking the time and trouble to consider a 'what else' beyond work, many have developed an impressive work/life balance which enables them to be clearer and more focused at work. Most pleasingly and surprisingly, perhaps, many have rediscovered the value in their relationships, partnerships and marriages, taking great pleasure in the time they spend with their families.

Hector Laing is by no means alone in considering the question 'And what else have I done or am I doing with my life?' The man or woman who is similarly unafraid to assess their inner motives and to take action will find themselves encountering a new pathway. And as they find within themselves incredible resources and the power to make a difference, their pathway will become broader and clearer. There is no greater contribution you can make, nothing more worthwhile or fulfilling, than to make a real difference to the lives of others.

There is a beautiful old Jewish teaching which says that,

just before a person dies, an angel comes to him or her from heaven to ask three questions:

- Tell me, is the world a better place because of your life?
- Is the world a better place because of the efforts you exerted?
- Is the world a better place because you were around?

I believe we would all like to be able to answer yes to all three questions.

chapter 11

How to Handle a Crisis

*I*t is easy, these days, to feel that everyone else out there is basking in the sunshine. The media constantly reinforce this image, encouraging us to chase after the 'perfect' lifestyle and picturing people who supposedly already live the ideal life. The fact is, though, that real life isn't all about sitting under a parasol sipping cool drinks in the sunshine, pleasant though this is – at least for a while. Real life is ups and downs, triumphs and setbacks, unexpected delights and unforeseen problems. And while anyone can sit under a parasol with a cool drink, the true test of our mettle is how we face the reverses and crises when they arrive.

The genuine person of character is the one who, when the wind begins to blow, turns bravely to face the wind and carries on. In fact the most successful life is often one in which the person concerned has faced more than their fair share of disappointment and loss, but has weathered it all. When you can take crisis in your stride, refuse to let rejection halt your progress and carry on in the face of defeat, then you have found true strength of character.

What is more, so often when we carry on against the odds relief appears just when we least expect it. In the bleakest and darkest of moments the sun does begin to shine through and help is at hand. The thirsty traveller struggling through the desert finds water over the brow of the next sand dune, or the shipwrecked mariner adrift in his small boat spots dry land at last. Successfully handling a crisis, no matter what its shape or form, requires a cool head, the ability to think clearly, strong determination and the wisdom to see the bigger picture and to understand that, however terrible, the crisis will pass.

KEEP YOUR COOL

Every one of us is tested many times. These tests, often in the form of crises, can arrive out of the blue and draw greatly on your resources and abilities. If you can come through a crisis with your nerve intact, your head high and the determination to move forward, then your confidence will soar because you will know that you can handle anything.

Handling a crisis often involves making tough decisions under pressure. But this doesn't mean making a decision without doubt or self-questioning. Keeping a cool head doesn't mean knowing all the answers ahead of time, or instant decision-making. On the contrary, doubt is an unavoidable part of such decision-making. But doubt needs to be dealt with before the decision is made, not afterwards.

Few people have a stronger reputation for keeping a cool head than former Mayor of New York Rudi Giuliani, who handled one of America's greatest crises with such cool and calm that everyone who met or saw him felt somehow reassured. When terrorists flew planes into New York's World Trade Center on 11 September 2001, killing almost five thousand people, Mayor Giuliani found all his strengths put to the test as he spoke from the stricken city to the rest of the world. In his book *Leadership* he says:

> A decisive leader can sometimes appear as though he never questions what his next move should be. Faced with tough decisions, I sometimes endure excruciating periods of doubt and soul-searching and, as I said, I always try to play out the results of each alternative. However, once I make the decision I move forward. Something clicks, and all my energies are applied to ensuring the decision works rather than fretting over whether it was the right one.

This point is vital. Once the decision is made, the person handling a crisis cannot afford to show doubt or to question whether the decision was right. Rather, he or she must put every effort into seeing the decision through to its conclusion. This is the essence of keeping your nerve and staying cool.

Field Marshal Montgomery, one of Britain's finest wartime military leaders, is another wonderful example of someone who could keep a cool head at times of extreme pressure.

> When General Montgomery was preparing for the decisive battle of El Alamein in 1942 he wore battledress and his characteristic black beret, ignoring all the usual trappings of generals. He instructed his staff that he would like to visit as many of the troops as he could. His mind must have been racing, his thoughts constantly focusing on the overall strategy and tactics of each and every division within his army, yet he appeared absolutely cool and calm.
>
> When he arrived at each location the troops were on parade awaiting him. On his instructions they would quickly gather round in an informal manner. Not for Monty any elaborate last-minute tactics or the 'throw

> something around the dressing room' approach of some of our more highly
> charged sporting coaches. Rather, having shown great pace of delivery,
> reassuring confidence and deeply disciplined self-control, he would
> conclude each short briefing by saying, 'Well, thank you, every one of you,
> for all your hard work in preparation. Now I don't know about you, but
> what I intend to do is get a good night's sleep!'

Monty knew that there was a time to hold back, to trust
that all had been done that could be done. He knew that
the best thing he could do was to give encouragement through
example, with his relaxed and calm approach. He would
have understood the words of another famous general, the
seventeenth-century Marquess of Montrose, who said, 'He
either fears his fate too much or his deserts are small who
puts it not unto the touch to win or lose it all.'

THE A AND E TEST

Handling a crisis means being willing to take the appropriate
and necessary action to resolve the situation. When critical
illness strikes or we have an accident we head for the nearest
hospital with an Accident and Emergency department. There
we trust that we will find confidence, expertise, reassurance
and help. At a time of business or personal crisis we need
the equivalent of an A and E department – our own personal
box of resources which we can call on to help the situation.
I call this the ability to agenda and empower.

Agenda and Empower

In the midst of a difficult situation, if you can agenda and
empower you can turn things around. First to set an agenda
for completion of the main task in hand and concentrate on
this, ignoring small difficulties. Then you will need to
empower others so that a feeling of ownership, purpose and

contribution is generated. Big decisions may be needed. It may be necessary to relocate or to diversify. Many of those who are affected may be afraid, since change always generates a certain amount of fear. This is the time when a leader must inspire confidence and trust and, through his or her own empowerment, empower others. When we stop feeling helpless we stop feeling hopeless and start to believe we can win through. If you feel that you have the power to change things, you feel hope and inspiration.

What holds certain leaders back from setting an agenda and empowering others in an 'accident and emergency' situation? Firstly, too much sunshine and ease can often impair quick-witted decision-making. Those who have been used to creaming off the perks while having to do relatively little will struggle when faced with a crisis. Secondly, there are those who hesitate because they feel the need to get everything absolutely right before acting or because they worry too much about what others will think of them. Hesitation of this kind can be disastrous and can ultimately sabotage the whole operation.

For when the time comes to face a crisis there will rarely be a perfect plan without hitches and disappointments or bumps and bruises along the way. Coping necessitates coming up with the best plan possible and then being willing to adapt and think on your feet as you go along. Ask any sea captain faced with the task of bringing his vessel home to port in gale force winds and high seas. It doesn't matter that some equipment, rigging or tackle may be lost along the way, or that the vessel itself may be damaged by flotsam and jetsam. No one will argue with that captain's decisions if the vessel and all those on board have been brought safely to dry land.

The ability to think carefully and clearly, to agenda and to empower, characterises not merely the strong and able person but also the person for whom the leadership moment has undoubtedly arrived.

> The textile manufacturing company in the north of England that had been in the same family for five generations began to see its life-blood flow away as a result of overseas competition – the market was being flooded with similar but cheaper items. Since it was now impossible to sustain costs and wages, it seemed that the end had come. After 150 years of providing jobs in their area, the company could not see a way to survive. That is, until a bright young manager stiffened the resolve and ailing confidence of his managing director, who was also his father. 'We can travel – we can find out how things are done over there and bring back the required expertise,' the young man insisted.
>
> And so they did, in a series of demanding and at times frustrating fact-finding trips from which they often returned exhausted and disconsolate. Yet they kept on going and eventually not only discovered new ideas and resources to strengthen their business at home, but also set up operations in other countries. The livelihoods of their employees were saved and the company began to thrive again. Just when the company appeared to have reached the point of exhaustion and many of those in charge wanted to give up, the energy and vision of the young manager had given the business a new lease of life.

At a time of great crisis for this firm, the young manager was able to agenda for change and to empower his managing director father and business colleagues to believe that, with new direction, new success could be achieved.

Here is another story which beautifully illustrates the ability to agenda and empower at a time of crisis. This time the crisis was in the construction industry. An imminent period of recession often reveals itself in this industry first, and seemingly powerful and successful companies can go to the wall overnight.

> Barr Construction was set up with eight employees in a joinery and, due to the determined leadership of their chief executive, Bill Barr, grew within thirty years to be a major player with more than a thousand employees and billboards across sites throughout the United Kingdom.
>
> Then came the threat of a particularly difficult period. Aware that things might get tough, in a spirit of corporate energy and endeavour Bill called his managers in for brainstorming sessions. The result was that they continued to develop road and house building yet found a niche market in the building of supermarket complexes and sports stadia. This new direction not only enhanced profits and visibility but kept many a Barr Construction household in work.
>
> None of this refocusing of activity would have been possible without the persistence and focus of Bill Barr. No one in the company knew that he was beginning to suffer from diabetes and increasing short-sightedness, yet he was prepared to travel extensively and to persevere wisely in an effort to help the company survive and thrive.

Bill Barr, like the young textile company manager, was able to agenda and empower in a crisis and so come through with flying colours.

THE COURAGE OF YOUR CONVICTIONS

When handling a crisis of any kind it is vital to have the courage of your convictions. If those around you are urging you in different directions, or you are facing several alternative ways to go forward, you need to be able to rely on your own strong inner voice. This is when knowing yourself really comes into its own, for when you know yourself, and your convictions and beliefs, you can stick with them no matter what. Without this self-knowledge you may be swayed by the loudest voices around you, which may not necessarily be the best.

The following story illustrates very powerfully the tough

choices which sometimes have to be made in a crisis and the need to stick with your convictions, even in the face of strong opposition.

In the USA, college sport is regarded very highly and operates at an astonishing level of expenditure. A recent survey revealed that Ohio State University and the University of Texas, for instance, each has sports budgets in the 50–60 million dollar range. Against this background one of the first tasks of any new college president or university principal is to make sure that there is a proper balance between academic performance and sporting success.

The newly appointed president of one university was well aware, as he drew up his strategic plan, that there were some outstanding football players among his students. And while he rated sporting success highly, the core values of courtesy and consideration for others, alongside good study habits, were the fundamentals of his vision for the university.

Soon after he arrived it was reported to him that one of the leading football players had, despite previous warnings, been loutish, rude and abusive towards members of the local community. Pressure was on the president from all sides. The football fanatics were pleading to keep this brilliant young footballer, but others wanted him thrown out. Everyone was watching the president with interest to see which way he would jump.

It was the first big test of his presidency. Faced with a very hard decision, he felt a strange mix of uncertainty and clarity. He felt strongly that his manifesto for courtesy and consideration for others must apply to the sporting as well as the academic programmes, but at the same time he knew that to expel this young footballer would cause an outcry.

However, he felt that he must set a clear example and informed the miscreant that he would have to leave. Then, at a hastily convened gathering of staff and students, he explained clearly the reasons for his decision. As he left there was considerable murmuring, and all too clearly he heard, 'He'll never get away with this.'

The next few days were a living hell. In all his months of preparation for his greatly valued position the new president had never considered having to act so decisively and controversially so early in his tenure. But he kept calm and, where appropriate, aloof, and soon the university community at every level began to get back to normal and to feel confident. They realised that in the new president they had a leader who was prepared to act conscientiously, carefully, and above all, as Rudyard Kipling put it, 'without fear or favour of the crowd'.

This college president, having deliberated long and hard over his decision, came through his first test with his integrity and self-belief intact. Once he had made up his mind he stuck by his decision without flinching, and others soon came to admire him for this. The most important factor here is that he acted from his convictions: he felt strongly that, although sporting success in university life is great, courteous behaviour on the part of the students is even greater.

Exercise: the Bottom Line Test

What is your bottom line? Are there certain values and principles about which you feel so strongly that compromise would be impossible? Knowing your own bottom line is vital to anyone facing a crisis. Of course there are always going to be, and should be, many areas in which compromise can be reached. Knowing your bottom line does not mean being rigid or inflexible. It simply means that you know yourself well enough to recognise the point beyond which you cannot accept compromise without betraying your own values. This knowledge will give you a sense of which direction to move in, no matter how tough the crisis.

Spend some time considering your personal bottom line. Ask yourself which values are most important to you, and at what stage you would need to stand firm in the face of opposition or demands for compromise.

THE PCC TEST

Many of my clients have made good use of this model when facing challenges and pressures. It is one which can be usefully applied in almost any situation, but is particularly useful at a time of crisis.

The PCC test is based on an institution which anyone who has lived in an English village will know well – the parochial church council. The PCC has a great deal of influence over village life. It is there to make decisions for the common good and to keep the village safe, functioning effectively and with a strong sense of community.

My PCC stands for pace, confidence and control, and like the English village PCC it focuses on the common good as well as on providing effective leadership. Maintaining pace, confidence and control will enable you to reach a good outcome in any situation.

Pace

Take a look at your pace and consider whether it is working for you. Are you rushing too much and missing vital information, or failing to listen to wise advice? Or are you being too slow, considering every aspect for far too long and missing the moment when you need to act? Decide whether you need to slow down or speed up a little. Try adjusting your pace, and see whether it feels more effective.

Confidence

What issues are getting in the way of your confidence? Are you allowing yourself to be too easily demoralised? Or are you overconfident, assuming that you are always right? A quiet, steady level of confidence is most effective. Remember situations in which you have achieved the desired outcome, or which have gone very well for you.

Encourage yourself and maintain a deep, genuine and unselfconscious confidence.

Control

Have you ever noticed how often discussions or negotiations break down when there is loss of control from either or both parties? Having control doesn't mean dictating the outcome – it means being confident enough to anticipate and appreciate the direction in which events are moving and to adapt accordingly.

> Often it takes an older and wiser colleague to point out our gifts and talents. Our fear of failure can kick in so readily and let us down. At a company's annual general meeting the wife of a former president approached the young chief executive to congratulate him on his performance. The CEO listened very carefully to this well-respected, highly talented and effective woman.
>
> 'When you came to the podium,' she said, 'there was a sense of reassurance, as if the members of the board and all the company members attending the AGM were really glad to have you there. That is something you should never forget in your future career. Your pace and confidence and control impressed us all.'
>
> The CEO acknowledged her praise and encouragement warmly and with gratitude. What the former president's wife did not know was that he had come to the AGM directly from a disciplinary hearing of a senior colleague, which was preying on his mind and to which he would shortly have to return. Greatly to his credit, his PCC had stood the test. His outer 'swan' had been calm and poised, although, in his own words, 'the legs were going like hell underneath'!

It is not surprising to learn that on such occasions, when a crisis is taking place and they are still required to present a calm, strong and reassuring front, our true leaders have looked back into their earlier lives for a source of strength, comfort and spiritual encouragement. The early Celtic followers of St Columba would often quote this blessing on departure or in anticipation of their particular leadership moments: 'The tongue of Columba be in my head, the eloquence of Columba be in my speech. The composure of the victorious Son of Grace be mine in the presence of the multitudes.'

UNEXPECTED HELP

At those times when you find yourself in the most dire and desperate of business or personal circumstances, it is comforting to remember that help can arrive unexpectedly and in the most unusual forms. Always be open to such help and, if all else seems to be failing you, look around for a person you can trust who might offer a helping hand.

The Parachute Regiment of the British Army, alongside the SAS, would claim to provide the very toughest military training, although this is often hotly disputed by the Royal Marines and other crack units such as the US Airborne Forces. In order to win the privilege of donning the red beret and wearing parachute wings a rigorous round of physical tests have to be passed. When I undertook this training myself it taught me two very clear lessons: first, that in each and every one of us there is more than we think; and second, that at really tough moments a word of comfort or a helping hand can make all the difference.

Most mornings were spent doing exercise after exercise in the gymnasium, followed perhaps by a ten-mile 'bash' across the muddiest of tank tracks, with further delights of physical hardship in the late afternoon and early evening! On one particular morning my nose had been hit by someone else's boot during an exercise on the ropes and I was struggling to breathe properly – I later discovered that it had been broken.

On return from the ten-mile 'bash' the sergeant major in charge of our squad halted us outside the swimming pool. 'Strip off everything and come inside,' was the order. Obeying orders to the letter, we left our clothes outside in the wet and cold. After a rapid workout on the trapeze we were ordered back outside to put on our clothes. I remembered longingly my mother's injunction never to put on damp clothes. Not quite the view of the Paras, though, who obviously thought soggy, damp clothes were character-building.

The squad marched back towards the depot, all of us growing colder, more miserable and dejected by the minute. We were running in file to order, getting closer and closer to the warm and peaceful haven of our barrack rooms, when the sergeant major abruptly ordered us to about turn and yelled, 'All right, then, let's go and do that all over again!'

At this point two fellow strugglers in front of me threw themselves on the ground in a heap with a barrage of swearing which, in polite form, would run along the lines of 'Stuff that for a game of soldiers.' I slowed down to a walk and almost did the same. That is, until a young recruit from the Royal Engineers, also training to be a Para, lifted my pack from behind and whispered in my ear, 'You're not going there, Padre. You can do this. We'll do it together.'

I have always been grateful to that young man. I was in the toughest circumstances of my life thus far, and without his intervention I would never have achieved my red beret and wings. In fact that unexpected lift from behind and the encouraging word in my ear shaped the rest of my life, because it taught me that at the worst moments there will always be help at hand.

LOOK TO THE FUTURE

When disaster has struck, what gives us back our hope is the ability to look to the future. There is always tomorrow, always another chance and a reason to go on. Nothing illustrates this better than a story I was told by Ron Neil, when he was Director of National and Regional Broadcasting at the BBC and I was the National Governor for Scotland.

On 13 March 1996, during a BBC Board of Governors meeting, a message came through that news was just breaking of a massacre in a primary school in the town of Dunblane in Scotland. Ron and I immediately left the meeting to travel north together. The BBC car in which we were driven to the airport was fitted with a television on which we were able to watch the news reports as they came in. As fellow Scots and fellow human beings we were devastated to learn that sixteen children and one teacher had been killed. When I turned to Ron, a very senior and experienced broadcasting executive, I saw that he was crying. Without taking his eyes off the television screen, he said, 'It's all so familiar.'

When I asked him why, he explained that when he was a young reporter with Radio 2, operating out of BBC Scotland in Glasgow, he was sent to cover the story of the Longhope lifeboat disaster in the Orkney Islands in January 1969. Ron remembered how in those days he had to file his story down the line from one of the traditional red GPO telephone boxes. He then went back into the local hotel where the entire community had gathered. Everyone there had a father or grandfather, son, husband or brother, relative or friend among the crew – no one was unaffected. The radio was on full blast, in the hope of any sightings or findings, when all of a sudden the news report that Ron had filed only moments earlier from the telephone box outside came across the airwaves to tell them that all eight men on board had been lost.

There was, as Ron recalled, silence for some considerable time, interspersed with the sobs of almost all who were present, irrespective of age or gender. That is, until a young boy stood up and broke the silence by saying, 'We've got to build another boat.'

And so they did. Not many years later Ron Neil found himself covering the dedication and launch of the new Longhope lifeboat in the presence of Queen Elizabeth, The Queen Mother. A service was held around the memorial to those who had died in the disaster. But no sooner had the minister announced the final hymn, 'Eternal Father, strong to save', which remembers 'those in peril on the sea', than ten oilskinned shoulders were tapped one by one. There had been a Mayday call, and the new lifeboatmen had to slip away from the service quickly.

> That young boy who courageously stood up in the hotel at the point of deepest despair was absolutely right. The work of saving lives at sea had to go on. As a community they simply had to look to the future.

As in life so in commerce and industry. For the clarity of thinking of that young boy in Orkney, substitute the knowledge, practice and expertise which come to those who are either in charge or have to take charge in a crisis. Squalls can threaten shipwreck, if not disaster. Often our best-laid schemes appear to founder on unforeseen rocks and the lifeline, for whatever reason, is not there. This is when we need to persevere, to build another boat and set sail again.

WHEN IT'S RIGHT TO KEEP GOING

All of us experience times when we wonder whether to keep going with a particular project or to give up and try something else. We all know the feeling of 'I'm so glad I stuck with it.' But how do you know, when crisis strikes, whether to stick with it or to write it off as a loss and divert your energy towards some other aim? The following guidelines can be of help when trying to make up your mind:

- Is the project something you really believe in? Do you believe it can succeed? Do you believe it is worthwhile? Do you feel 100 per cent behind it?
- Is the project entirely consistent with your own values and aims? Is it something you can argue for with passion and conviction even in your lowest, most tired and dispirited moments?
- Can you picture a successful outcome and see, broadly speaking, what is needed to reach it?
- If it is a group or corporate endeavour, do others believe in it too?
- Is this something for which others are now looking to you for leadership and direction?

If you can answer yes to all these questions, it is well worth persisting. If the answer to any of the questions is no, ask yourself why. Then consider what might need changing, adjusting or redirecting in order to reach a yes, or whether it is truly time to let go and apply your energy elsewhere.

> When the manufacturing company hit a major crisis – the cost of raw materials had doubled and buyers were in short supply – the young managing director was determined to save the business and carry on. Yet despite the view of the board that the future looked hopeless, he persuaded the staff to take a pay cut and worked tirelessly to keep output going and to find new clients for the company's products.
>
> After three months things were looking no better, but when the MD arrived at yet another board meeting he was still looking defiant and determined to carry on. However, by the end of that meeting he had found the courage to change his mind. To carry on was simply unfair to the employees and ultimately a waste of energy. Sadly, he returned to tell the workforce that the company must close. He had made every effort, but he had become increasingly isolated in his efforts and it was clear that the miracle solution he had hoped for was not about to present itself.

To re-evaluate can sometimes be the toughest option. None the less it is important to look at things regularly and objectively in order to determine whether it really is worth going on.

BEYOND THE CRISIS

All crises come to an end. In fact the very nature of crisis means that it is almost always short-lived. And having drawn on all your resources, self-knowledge and experience to carry you through the difficulties, the aftermath is a time for drawing breath and reviewing. It is important to ask yourself, and others concerned, the following questions:

- Could anything have been done to avert the crisis in the short term?
- Was the crisis handled in the best possible way?
- What lessons have been learned from it?
- What could be done to prevent a similar crisis in the future?

Although crises can't usually be avoided altogether, no business or organisation wants to be permanently lurching from one crisis to the next. It is vital to think ahead and plan for the unexpected, so that all the available energy and resources can be used for truly unavoidable occurrences rather than those which may be the result of carelessness or lack of planning. And when attention has been paid to the details, when lessons have been recorded and learned from previous experiences so as to prepare as well as possible for foreseeable outcomes, crises will be rare.

chapter 12

From
Captivity
to Freedom

One of the most moving experiences of my life was spending time with my family on Robben Island, off the sea coast of Cape Town in South Africa. Our afternoon there, however, hardly compares with the 'long walk to freedom' of Nelson Mandela, the first black President of South Africa, who spent twenty-seven years in captivity, nine of them on Robben Island.

Before our trip to Robben Island we visited the Nelson Mandela Foundation Gallery. There we saw the following words, written by Mandela to accompany a set of his sketches of Robben Island:

Today when I look at Robben Island I see it as a celebration of the struggle and a symbol of the finest qualities of the human spirit, rather than as a monument to the brutal tyranny and oppression of apartheid.

> Robben Island is a place where courage endured in the face of endless hardship, a place where people kept on believing when it seemed their dreams were hopeless, and a place where wisdom and determination overcame fear and human frailty.
>
> It is true that Robben Island was once a place of darkness, but out of that darkness has come a wonderful brightness, a light so powerful that it could not be hidden behind prison walls, held back by prison bars or hemmed in by the surrounding sea.
>
> In these sketches entitled 'My Robben Island' I have attempted to colour the Island sketches in ways that reflect the positive light in which I view it. This is what I would like to share with people around the world and, hopefully, also project the idea that even the most fantastic dreams can be achieved if we are prepared to endure life's challenges.

As we were leaving the exhibition I spotted four striking sculptures, larger versions of which will one day be proudly raised on Robben Island. They represent the four stages of the struggle against apartheid personified so clearly by the life of Nelson Mandela: captivity, dialogue, community and freedom. The beauty of these sculptures and the power of what they represent struck me very deeply. For, just as they personify the struggle towards freedom under apartheid, they can also be applied to the journey towards awareness and understanding which each one of us undertakes in our lives.

CAPTIVITY

Often we can be hemmed in by our personal circumstances or barred from creativity by the agenda of others. Many people who are struggling in their working or business lives will understand this scenario. Captivity can come about either from external forces or from the agenda we set ourselves from within.

What are your captivities? What is holding you back? Are there negative influences from your childhood and youth which are restraining or restricting you? Have your inner core values become detached from your actions and expectations? Are you living the life according to the prescriptions and proscriptions of others, rather than letting the inner reality of your soul express itself through what you set out to do in life?

DIALOGUE

It was only when Nelson Mandela and his fellow black political activists Walter Sisulu and Robert Sobukwe began a dialogue with other political figures in the anti-apartheid movement such as the incomparable Joe Slovo, the Lithuanian Jewish immigrant who was later to hold office in Mandela's first government, that the struggle against South Africa's repressive racist regime started to grow in national and international strength. So often we fail to realise the benefit of dialogue, through lack of confidence in making ourselves clear or through fear that others will not listen or understand us. The celebrated poet David Whyte, who lectures extensively on bringing the soul and personality back into the workplace, has regularly and courageously suggested to the corporate world that conversation is where strength of character develops. It is through vulnerability in conversation that personal growth begins. It is through a sense of openness in dialogue that self-discovery and realisation can truly begin, sometimes with the most unlikely people and in the most unlikely places.

COMMUNITY

Sometimes we hear people – and not necessarily old people – wistfully recalling how things were in times past and lamenting how things have changed. Those feelings often relate to a sense of community which the person concerned believes existed in the past but no longer does so.

Speed of communication and ease of travel have indeed fragmented communities. Nowadays people can live quite anonymously, with no knowledge or understanding of their neighbours.

Pace of change and the drive for short-term results have brought about a similar cultural change in the workplace, too. The young Australian banker with two toddlers and a wife expecting number three felt that he could only enjoy the pleasure of his family away from work, because he imagined no one would be interested. The fact is that almost everyone would have been interested had he been able to break free from this particular self-imposed captivity, to engage in dialogue and so to bring with him to his working life a sense of community.

The Oscar-winning film *Local Hero* portrays a Scottish community faced with the prospect of an oil terminal being built there, bringing with it lucrative compensation and seeming prosperity but at the same time threatening to destroy the existing culture of a small community. Then the Texan oil baron, played by Burt Lancaster, arrives to spend some time in the hut of the beach-combing landowner and a different type of communal wellbeing is experienced and shared. Until that point Burt Lancaster's character has been working from the outside in, and his rich discovery during the course of the film is of the integrity which works from the inside out.

FREEDOM

When you work from the inside out rather than from the outside in, an indescribable feeling of freedom can be experienced. In captivity Nelson Mandela discovered his own inner soul and was able to turn the darkness of that period into the light of the new rainbow nation of South Africa. In his own words, 'even the most fantastic dreams can be achieved if we are prepared to endure life's challenges'.

What Nelson Mandela and the four sculptures represent is this: we can face our own captivities with courage, and through dialogue arrive at a sure sense of community in our own souls and in the souls of others, so that ultimately we can experience a deep sense of freedom.

AN OPEN HEART

The person of wisdom and principle is the man or woman who is unafraid to assess existing inner motives, to encounter a new pathway and to share what they have in order to make a real difference to the lives of others – both in the workplace and beyond. The journey to freedom, the journey I hope you have begun through this book and will continue long after you have put it down, is therefore one which must be travelled with an open heart. An abiding principle of mine has been this: if you can endeavour to operate in a spirit of integrity and with an open heart, then no matter what the circumstances or the disappointments or the fears or failures in your life, you will find the courage to keep on going towards your goals. If you can do that and keep on being inspired to get back on your feet and stay on the road, then very often you will find companions on your route. And, most delightfully and surprisingly of all, you will find others travelling towards you to meet you and to greet you.

As my great-grandfathers knew so well, we need to discover who we are and what we have in common with others – not what separates us. Too many people are indoctrinated by churches and politics to allow their differences to be bigger than their similarities. I believe that we should all be striving for our common humanity, and that if we do so we will be better and stronger together. We all live in multi-cultural, multi-faith societies, and we need to celebrate this through our acceptance of one another.

The person with self-knowledge will discover his or her empathy with fellow human beings and make this the cornerstone of success. This person hears the word 'no' and thinks 'why not?' He or she is not afraid to think big, to break down barriers and to innovate.

When Cliff Morgan, the legendary Wales and British Lions rugby player who went on to become head of BBC Radio Sport, spoke at a rugby dinner some years ago, he said, 'The greatest challenge in life today is how we deal with greed and mediocrity.' He went on to outline how, in sport as in work and in life in general, these two negative qualities have indeed got in the way.

It is greed and mediocrity which create corporate and personal failure and disaster on the scale of the Enron scandal, and on a smaller scale all around us. But the self-aware person will choose courage and integrity over greed and mediocrity every time. It is only when we move beyond personal greed and aspire to more than mediocrity that we can be released from our captivities to the freedom of knowing who we are and what we want to do with the rest of our lives.

LET THE LIGHTS COME ON

Cliff Morgan went on in that speech to describe how, when he had been interviewing the actress Liv Ullman, he had asked her, 'When was it that you realised you could become a great actress?' Her reply was simple and to the point: 'I think it was at one stage when I was surrounded by my family and friends and greatest supporters. It was then that I felt that I could do it. It was almost as if the lights came on.'

I hope that, after reading this book, the lights of self-knowledge and self-awareness that lead towards brave and responsible leadership have indeed come on for you. Such leadership, as the remedy that we bring to areas of dis-ease in our life and in our work, has revitalised businesses, communities and families. As Nelson Mandela famously said in his inaugural speech as President of South Africa, 'Your playing small doesn't serve the world. There is nothing enlightening about shrinking so that other people around you won't feel insecure. We are all meant to shine as children do. And as we let our light shine, we unconsciously give other people permission to do the same.' This is the true art of leadership: giving yourself permission to shine, and then, through your own actions, beliefs and example, giving others permission to shine too.

HODDER
MOBIUS

Transform your life
with Hodder Mobius

For the latest information on the best in
Spirituality, Self-Help,
Health & Wellbeing and Parenting,

visit our website
www.hoddermobius.com